SPAIN

CUISINES OF THE WORLD

SPAIN

CORNELIA ROSALES DE MOLINO

Recipe photographs: Foodphotography Eising

THUNDER BAY
P·R·E·S·S

France

Galicia
Asturias
Canta-bria
Basque Country
Navarre
Léon
La Rioja
Andorra
Old Castile
Aragón
Catalonia
Madrid
Portugal
Extre-madura
Castile-La Mancha
Valencia
Balearic Islands
Murcia
Andalucía
Canary Islands
Morocco
Algeria
Morocco

CONTENTS

SPAIN: LAND OF FIESTAS

Spain conjures up images of sun, sea, and color; of the white Mediterranean beaches and the dusty ocher heartlands; of the snow-capped peaks of the Pyrenees and the orange groves of Valencia. Don Quixote, Carmen, Flamenco, siestas,

and bullrings are facets of a distinctive culture that combines romance and spectacle, drama and ceremony, excitement and relaxation. At its heart lies an exuberant appetite for enjoying life, witnessed by a multitude of religious and secular fiestas. Processions and pilgrimages, fireworks and dancing celebrate anything from a successful harvest to Spain's 15th-century deliverance from its Moorish invaders.

A somewhat festive approach is also a characteristic of everyday life. Typically Spain keeps much later hours than other European countries. The evening meal is eaten at any time up to midnight. A lively group of people might gather round a table beneath an arbor outside a restaurant, their children romping about without anyone bothering to tell them to sit still.

Fiesta or otherwise, food and drink are central to Spanish life. A traditional day would begin with a rather meager breakfast, no more than a cup of coffee and a few cookies, say, or a visit to a pavement café or a churrería for churros, long, crisp, hot donuts, piped through a forcing-bag into boiling oil and deep-fried. Lunch at home with the family, in contrast, would be a more lavish affair, starting around 2 p.m. and often continuing into the late afternoon.

Tapas time begins around 7 p.m. Tapas are a wide range of appetizers that are offered by bars for customers to nibble as they sip their sherry, wine or beer. These distinctive Spanish snacks help stave off hunger until the evening

meal, which is rarely served before 9 p.m.

Finally, it is back to the bar in which the evening began to drink strong coffee or a glass of brandy.

To a large extent, of course, the leisurely midday meal has now gone the way of the afternoon siesta. Office workers in Madrid are accustomed, as are those elsewhere in the world, to grabbing a quick bite at lunchtime; families have less time to lavish on their daily meal. The culinary traditions endure, however. Weekends and feast days still follow time-honored patterns, bringing together family and friends to enjoy authentic Spanish cuisine.

This book tells you how to make your own delicious Spanish meals at home. The first chapter is an introduction to the country, its widely varied regions and the corresponding local dishes, produce, and festivals. Then come authentic recipes from all over Spain for everything from tapas and soups to desserts and pastries, arranged in the sequence in which they are traditionally served. There are recommendations for wine, notes on some of the more important ingredients, and, where necessary, step-by-step photographs to explain more complex techniques. The glossary defines some of the less common terms and ingredients used in Spanish cookery and menu suggestions allow you to combine dishes in authentic meals that will conjure up a flavor of Spain at your own table. As the Spanish say, "Buen provecho."

A COUNTRY OF MANY LANDS

The Spanish traditionally speak of their land in the plural, as Las Españas, reflecting a diversity of cultures that embraces four languages and many regions and nations.

Culinary traditions share the same regional differences, reflecting Spain's location between Europe and Africa, its varied geography, and its rich history.

The Iberian Peninsula, of which Spain occupies the largest part, was described by the English poet, W.H. Auden as "A fragment nipped off hot Africa, soldered so crudely to inventive Europe." And, indeed, the baked red hills of the southern interior could be part of Africa, though the lush green valleys of Galicia in the northwest might be in Ireland. Spanish cookery reflects this hybrid character: the sweet or spicy dishes of Andalucía echo the climate and tastes of North Africa, while the warming stews of the Atlantic coast conjure images of temperate Europe.

North and south are separated by an interior which is largely rugged and inhospitable – Spain is Europe's most mountainous country after Switzerland. The weather of the vast brown plateau at its heart, the Meseta, is described as "Three months of winter and nine months of hell." Around this tableland are the mountains, through which a few unnavigable rivers wind, which kept the regions isolated from each other, just as the Pyrenees kept Spain largely cut off from the rest of Europe.

Along with geography, Spanish cooking has been shaped by the history of the peninsula, which has long attracted conquerors. The Ancient Greeks, Romans, Celts, Carthaginians, and Phoenicians all left traces of their influence. But the greatest legacy is that of the Moors, the Moslems of North Africa who ruled much of Spain from the 8th through the 13th century, and who were not completely defeated by the Spaniards until the 15th century. Citrus fruits, almonds, and spices such as saffron and cumin are just some of their contributions to Spanish cuisine.

When Columbus discovered America in 1492, he heralded the arrival of Spain's Siglo de oro or Golden Age, when spoils from the New World made the country rich and powerful. The explorers brought back a wealth of unknown spices, and Spain's new grandeur was reflected in culinary advances. This period saw the highpoint of Spanish haute cuisine: it set the standards throughout Europe, and other European rulers even imported Spanish chefs.

It is regional cookery, however, that remains the heart of authentic Spanish cuisine. Fish and seafood dominate the Atlantic coast; game and roast meats are the traditional fare of the center; Valencia's paddies yield rice for paella. Local specialties make the most of local ingredients and traditions, combining in a rich cuisine that reflects the many-faceted nature of a complex country.

In their Sunday best, the men of the Galician fishing village of Malpica escort a statue of their patron saint, Nuestra Señora de Carme (Our Lady of the Carmel), across the harbor. The ceremony, held each summer, is to ensure an abundant catch from these rich waters.

Galicia, Asturias, and Cantabria

The soil and the sea dominate the cuisine of "green Spain," so-called because of the fertility of its rain-watered earth. The region has long been attractive to settlers. Cave paintings in Altamira, Cantabria, and Tito Bustillo in Asturias are the legacy of inhabitants of some 15,000 years ago. Around 1000 B.C., the Celts overran what is now Galicia, in Spain's far-flung northwestern corner. They found a mild climate and a mist-cloaked, hilly landscape that was more reminiscent of their northern homelands than of the arid Spanish heartland or the Mediterranean coast.

Today, the area is covered with tiny fields, stone walls, and slate roofs. Every square yard of available land, including man-made terraces cut into the slopes of the inland mountains, is covered with strips of crops – wheat, potatoes, tomatoes, and beans. Isolated from the rest of Spain by rugged peaks, the Galicians retain traces of their Celtic origins. Traditional dances here are accompanied by the bagpipes, which are unknown in the rest of Spain.

Asturias and Cantabria, too, are cut off by the towering ranges of the Cantabrian Cordilleras and the Picos de Europa that run parallel to the coast. Their spectacular scenery of snow-capped peaks, deep gorges, forested slopes, and lush meadows is reminiscent of the Alps.

The cows that graze on the lush mountain pastures in summer provide some of Spain's best veal, and their creamy milk is used for such dishes as the renowned Asturian rice pudding and the thick cornmeal mush that is a characteristic local breakfast. The area also produces Spain's answer to Roquefort cheese, the creamy, mild, blue-veined Cabrales, wrapped in tree leaves and ripened like Roquefort in limestone caves.

Cereal crops are important here. All over Asturias and Galicia, there are long narrow grain stores, or *hórreos*. Built on short stone stilts to protect their contents from rodents and damp, these distinctive buildings are usually topped with crosses, so that they resemble tiny churches.

Asturias is renowned for *fabada*, a warming stew of large white beans and smoked sausage, which provides an antidote to the long and rainy winters. Like other mountainous areas, the region produces fine pork and ham. Even salmon and trout might be cooked in smoked pork fat in this region. Beans are also combined with rabbit, partridge, or mussels to create unusual but flavorsome dishes.

The Atlantic Ocean offers a range of treasures, which are harvested by Spain's important fishing industry. The wild granite shores of the Bay of Biscay yield abundant fish and shellfish for regional dishes, such as stuffed squid cooked in its own ink. *Vieiras*, large, fleshy scallops weighing up to one pound from the fjordlike inlets on Galicia's western coast called *rías* are a special delicacy. (The fluted scallop shell was the traditional emblem of the thousands of pilgrims who made their way along El Camino de Santiago, the Way of St. James. This ancient pilgrimage route across Europe ends in the Galician town of Santiago de Compostela, where the relics of St. James the Apostle are preserved in a magnificent cathedral.)

Vieiras are usually oven-baked in their shells with a crisp, herb crust. In contrast, Galicians prefer to sauté other shellfish in a little oil, so as to retain the intense saltwater flavor.

A favorite dessert is *Tocino de cielo* (bacon from heaven), a light and creamy egg dessert. Known all over Spain, it is served here doused with cider, the chief drink of Asturias. The province is ill-suited for grape-growing, but the golden, slightly sparkling and rather strong cider is drunk with meals in place of wine, and is also used for cooking. It is found at its best in a *chigra* or cider-house, drawn sparkling fresh straight from the barrel.

As befits a region where shellfish rule, the best wine in neighboring Galicia is white. The light, tangy Albariño goes wonderfully with fish and seafood. The authentic way to drink it is from traditional conchas, simple white china goblets, which can be found in markets in towns such as La Coruña.

Festivals

In September, the town of Oviedo celebrates the Feast of St. Matthew with bullfights and a parade of decorated floats. The highlight of the year at Santiago de Compostela is the week-long Festival of St. James, which

begins on July 25 with a huge firework display in the cathedral square.

High spirits in a Galician farmer's wife expressing her joy at the harvest. Good crops are crucial for Galicia's many small, traditional farms.

The waters of the Atlantic lie deceptively still beyond the tiny harbor of Ea, near Guernica, in the Basque Country. Long sea walls form a harbor to shelter boats during the Bay of Biscay's notorious storms.

The Basque Country and Navarre

The Basque Country – rich in natural ingredients and with a culture that traditionally places great emphasis on excellence in cookery – is sometimes reckoned to be home to Spain's best cuisine. Hilly, green, damp, and wooded, this is a well-farmed region of orchards and lush cattle pastures. Blinding fogs sweep suddenly south off the Bay of Biscay to cloak the land in mist; equally suddenly, the gloom is broken by the sun. The region is in part densely populated, especially round such

Built for convenience right to the water's edge, traditional houses line the harbor of the small fishing village of Pasajes de San Juan, in the Basque province of Guipúzcoa.

industrial centers as Bilbao and Vitoria.

Neighboring Navarre, dominated in the north by the lonely peaks of the Pyrenees and in the south running down to foothills and steppes, is also home to part of the ancient Basque race; the rest live on the far side of the Pyrenees in France. The different groups of this fiercely independent people are united by a unique culture, and by Euskera, their shared language, unrelated to any other known tongue.

The mountain streams of Navarre are full of firm-fleshed salmon and the trout that go to make the renowned *Truchas a la navarra*, whole trout stuffed with serrano ham and pan-fried. Nearer the coast, people prefer their fish and shellfish from the cold, blue-gray waters of the Bay of Biscay. Among the most popular ways of preparing fish are *a la vasca* (Basque-style), with wine and green vegetables and *a la vizcaina* (Vizcaya-style) with a combination of sweet and hot peppers.

Mild sweet peppers are also an important ingredient in the traditional *Piperrada*, a colorful omelet in which they are combined with ham. Another characteristic local vegetable is thick, succulent asparagus. The inland woods harbor wild boar, hare, rabbit, and all kinds of game birds.

As well as their fish dishes, Basque cooks are famous for sauces. Among the most delicious are the garlicky *pilpil*, or the green *salsa verde* made with peas and flavored with parsley. Other sauces often offer very distinctive flavors, containing unusual ingredients such as cinnamon or unsweetened chocolate.

The local cheese is mild, buttery Idiázabal made from ewe's milk, which has a delicate, smoky flavor and is often served with nuts or used for cakes and desserts. Candies from the region include pastillas, delicious caramels from Pamplona, and chocolate truffles from Vitoria.

As for wine, a delicate red Alavesa, from the most northerly part of the Rioja wine-growing area, is light enough to be drunk throughout a meal. Better with fish, perhaps, is the Basque Chacolí, which is tangy and slightly sparkling. Pacharán, a fruity sloe liqueur, served ice-cold, is a delightful finishing touch to a meal, as reflected in the popularity it has found recently all over the rest of Spain.

The traditions of local cuisine are preserved in special gastronomic societies that raise food to the level of a Basque national sport. Entirely male, they have their own clubhouses where members meet regularly to try out new recipes and test the results. The high spot of the culinary year is the annual banquet of the gastronomic societies in San Sebastián on the evening of January 19, at which nonmembers are also welcome. Celebrations continue the next day, the feast of the town's patron saint, when to the beat of drums, processions of bakers and cooks make their way through the streets and until late into the night the city becomes a gourmet's paradise.

Festivals

The most famous and exhilarating of the region's festivals is the San Fermín fiesta in Pamplona in July, where young men dressed in white, with scarlet berets and scarves, run bulls through the streets. The human participants are traditionally allowed only a rolled-up newspaper with which to defend themselves.

Massive sandstone outcrops of the Pyrenees tower over the village of Riglos. The bizarre formations of the soft rock are the results of millennia of erosion by the wind and rain.

A fisherman mends his nets in the busy port of Palamós on the Costa Brava. The so-called "wild coast" stretches north from Barcelona to the French border.

Catalonia

For many of the tourists who visit the Costa Brava in large numbers every year, Catalonia is package-tour Spain, but this historic region has much more to offer. Behind the warm, subtropical coast, on which palm trees and citrus fruits flourish, lie rugged mountains that cut the region off from the rest of Spain. Historically, Catalonia has been more closely tied to southern France than to the Spanish heartland; the Catalan language, mother tongue of five million people, resembles the old *langue d'oc* of France more than Castilian Spanish.

Isolation has fostered a distinctive and independent Catalan culture, celebrated by artists such as Salvador Dalí and Joan Miró, and by the architect Antonio Gaudí whose Art Nouveau buildings characterize the regional capital of Barcelona.

The city is home to one of the most characteristic celebrations of Catalan culture. On Sunday mornings, scores of people gather outside the Cathedral of Santa Eulalia and join hands to perform the *sardana*, a traditional dance accompanied by wind instruments and small drums. The natural riches that are the basis of Catalan cooking come together in Barcelona's magnificent Art Nouveau market-hall, La Boquería, grouped by color in mouth-watering displays. There are olives, fresh fruits and vegetables; sardines and monkfish freshly caught by the fishing fleet; in the fall, there are wild mushrooms called *rovellon*, a prized Catalan delicacy; and partridge, quail, and hare are contributed by hunters from the region's wilderness.

Catalonia is a land of geographical contrasts. To the north of Barcelona there is the Costa Brava, or "wild" coast, with its rocky cliffs and small inlets, while to the south of the city lie the long, golden beaches of the Costa Dorada. The slopes of the Pyrenees are thickly timbered but the flatter land below is heavily cultivated with grain, vines, olives, fruits, and vegetables.

Contrast also characterizes Catalan cuisine. At its heart is a thrifty waste-not, want-not attitude plus a creativity that can result in unusual combinations of ingredients. The so-called "land and sea" dishes, for example, combine meat and seafood most other cooks would keep strictly separate: chicken and lobster in a hazelnut sauce, say, or rabbit with squid and shrimp.

A market in Barcelona provides a colorful display of Catalonia's abundant vegetables, fruit, fish, and meat.

Of the many imaginative fish dishes of the coast, the most renowned is *zarzuela*. In this so-called "operetta" of seafood, several fish and shellfish are combined in a stew with a subtle sauce of wine, tomatoes, and saffron, whose flavors enhance rather than overwhelm the distinctive taste of each fish.

Sauces are an important element in Catalan cooking, and are often hotter and spicier here than elsewhere in Spain. *Romesco*, made from cayenne pepper or paprika, oil, almonds, and sometimes tomatoes, is equally with grilled or broiled fish or meats. *Samfaina* is a thick and spicy vegetable sauce similar to *ratatouille*; it too can accompany meat or fish, but goes particularly well with poultry.

The classic Catalan dessert is *crema catalana*. This is a rich but light egg and milk custard resembling *crème brûlée*, with a thin crust of caramelized sugar, traditionally crystallized with a special red-hot iron just before serving.

A suitable drink to accompany the region's savory specialties is a dry Catalonian white wine. The wines of Penedés, just south of Barcelona, are particularly fine, as are those from Alella, which also produces smooth reds. Catalonia, and especially Sant Sadurní de Noya, is the center for the production of Cava, the name given to sparkling white wines made by the champagne method; though differing in taste, they make a good alternative.

Festivals

In Barcelona, the Midsummer's Eve celebrations on June 23 center around a huge bonfire on Montjuic, the hill that overlooks the port. Also in the city, the festival of Our Lady of Mercy, from September 24 through 28, is an occasion for bullfighting, folk dancing, and a music festival. Around the same time, further down the coast in the town of Tarragona, the feast of St. Thecla is marked by folk dances and human pyramid contests.

Brightly colored mosaic covers the 70-foot high "Dona i Ocell" Woman and Bird a sculpture by Joan Miró in a Barcelona park. Miró, a world renowned 20th-century Catalan artist, is held in special esteem in the city of his birth.

In traditional finery, women in La Alberca celebrate the feast of the Assumption with a mystery play. Such plays have been performed since medieval times all over Europe.

Soft sunshine falls on the 16th-century cloister of the convent of Las Dueñas in Salamanca, and the cathedral beyond. Since 1218, the city has been home to one of Spain's finest universities.

Old Castile and León

Old Castile and León are the historic heart of Spain. These are regions of endless horizons, with villages scattered among plains of wheat and rye in the north and farms of sheep and fighting bulls in the south. The earth is dry and cracked, either by ice or heat, all year round.

In contrast to the desolation of the unpopulated tracts of the Meseta plateau are the glories of the cities, which recall a rich past. There are walled Avila, Spain's highest and coldest provincial capital, for example, or Segovia with its fairy-tale castle and the world's finest working Roman aqueduct. The warrior El Cid, hero of the campaign against the Moors, is buried in Gothic Burgos, while Plaza Mayor in Salamanca, a medieval city of spires and domes, is one of the finest squares in all Spain.

Like the cities, the cuisine has the flavor of a bygone age. It is hearty and sustaining, a fortification against the brutal elements of land and sky. Meals often consist of roast meats cooked in old bakers' ovens over a wood fire of gorse, thyme, or vine cuttings to impart an aromatic flavor. Baby lamb and suckling pig are killed much younger than elsewhere in Europe, making them very tender: "You can cut them with the edge of a plate," a saying goes. Waiters and cooks sometimes still do this, revealing juicy, pale-colored flesh beneath the crisp, dry skin. In the many restaurants based in old castles or monasteries, lit by torches or candles, such dishes are in perfect keeping with the medieval atmosphere.

Accompaniments for the copious meats are as simple as the roasts. There is the much-loved Spanish omelet confusingly called a *tortilla*. It is served either as a plain potato omelet or in a gourmet version with green asparagus, tender ham, or even shrimp. Pulses –

The perfectly preserved walls that surround Avila in Castile are as forbidding today as in the 11th century when they were built to protect the city from the Moors. The walls are 1 ½ miles long, 40 feet high, and 10 feet thick. They have 88 towers and nine fortified gates.

beans of all shapes and colors, used both fresh and dried, and garbanzo beans or chickpeas – are also frequently featured. Served all over Spain, they are essential to Castilian cuisine, where they are the basis of the many versions of the stew called *cocido*. They are also eaten boiled, roasted, and salted to make a tasty snack, and sold by the bag at every street festival or fair.

The specialty of the city of León is a highly seasoned, creamy garlic soup. During the festival of St. Peter and St. Paul, in late July, it is cooked in huge cauldrons in the market square and served free to revelers.

Another local celebration is "trout week." The Cantabrian mountains in the north of the region have rivers and streams which yield what are reputed to be the best trout in all Spain. Every August, León celebrates with angling competitions, cookery demonstrations, and great feasts at which trout are eaten "fisherman-style" – packed in clay and

baked in the embers of an open fire.

A favorite treat is *yemas*, golden-yellow candies made from egg yolks. The best come from Avila and make a delicious souvenir.

Either side of Valladolid, there are the thriving wine-growing areas of Rueda and La Ribera del Duero. Rueda, known for its sherry-like wines, now also produces refreshing, tangy whites; La Ribera del Duero's dry reds have a velvety quality. Other regional wines include the fruity reds from El Bierzo north of León and the heavier, dark reds of the Toro area further south.

Festivals

Segovians enjoy a reputation for gaiety, exemplified each February by the festival of Santa Agüeda, when women in traditional costumes take over the running of the province's villages. At the end of June, the city celebrates the feast of St. John and St. Peter with folk dancing and medieval ballads.

The vacation village of Torla is dominated by the towering outcrops of the Pyrenees. Torla lies at the entrance of Ordesa y Monte Perdido, one of Spain's finest national parks, and is a popular base for hikers.

Aragón and La Rioja

Aragón, whose northern border lies among the high peaks of the Pyrenees, was once a powerful medieval kingdom whose dominion stretched as far as Naples and the island of Sicily. The Moorish architecture of Zaragoza, the former capital, reflects a history of conflict and domination. The city stands in the midst of lush orchards and truck farms, but the appearance of fertility is deceptive. Only large-scale irrigation, with canals fed by the Ebro and other rivers, has made the one-time desert turn green.

Beyond the valleys lie the bleak, thinly populated plains of the Meseta plateau. Northwest of Aragón, La Rioja, Spain's premier wine district, has a bare highland feel, with vineyards, crops, and pasture alternating on the stony ground.

This harsh land has its own natural treasures. The emphasis here is on game. In the Pyrenees the mountain streams are full of fish, especially trout, and there are rich game reserves on the densely wooded slopes. As in other mountainous areas, sheep, goats, and pigs are the characteristic domestic animals. La Rioja is the home of *chorizo*, a traditional smoked sausage which is renowned throughout Spain.

In general, the cuisine is hearty rather than refined. Trout are usually cooked quite simply, either fried or broiled; before cooking, however, they may be stuffed with ham, which makes them remarkably tasty. Lamb, kid, and game are combined with aromatic herbs in the versatile shepherd's stew known as *Cordero a la pastora*.

In contrast, finely blended sauces are the basis of many dishes in Aragón, which belongs to the so-called "zona de los chilindrones." *Chilindrón* is the name of both a card game and a popular local sauce, though there is no clear connection between the two. The sauce, a pungent, slowly simmering blend of tomatoes, onions, garlic, and red bell peppers, with added ingredients such as serrano ham, chili peppers, or saffron, suits practically any kind of meat, from tender little squab to heavy mutton.

The accompaniment to such dishes, essential for mopping up the sauce, is *migas*. These crisply roasted dice of garlic bread resembling croûtons are the color of rust and are flavored with paprika or hot pepper, or sometimes ham. Said to constitute the most ancient dish in the whole Iberian peninsula, migas are eaten everywhere in Spain, at any time of day, and with anything from meat sauces and fried vegetables to fruit and even chocolate! The best bread for making them is the typical round, flat loaves baked in the wood-burning ovens or *panaderías* of small-town bakeries.

Zaragoza is famous for all kinds of mouth-watering cakes and pastries and for a range of tempting confectionery such as bittersweet marzipan.

The best accompaniment to any meal is a local wine. In Aragón, for example, there is the potent, dark red, violet-scented Cariñena. The center of the wine production for the region, and for the whole of Spain, is La Rioja, the land along the Ebro River northwest of Aragón. Its vintages are often compared with those of Bordeaux, and its present high quality and worldwide reputation owes much to French winemakers who came here from Bordeaux in the 19th century to escape the phylloxera pest that was attacking their own vines.

La Rioja, though possessing a more upland character than the French were used to – the best vineyards are 1500 feet above sea level – provided good growing conditions. Low vines all-

purpose flourished in a climate that was milder than in much of Spain, with plentiful rain and relatively short summers and winters. Before the French eventually returned home, they had established their wine-growing traditions and expertise which were previously lacking in Spain.

The main growing area is centered around the town of Haro. The finest Rioja wines are soft, fruity reds with a taste of oak from the Rioja Alavesa, which are lighter in color than most Spanish wines; light reds (formerly called Claretes) are drier and lighter bodied. Of the white Riojas, the dry whites are crisp and lively, and generally better than sweeter dessert wines.

Festivals

In October, the town of Zaragoza stages the Pilar Festival in honor of the Virgin of Pilar, patron saint of all Spain, with processions of giant lanterns paraded through the streets on wagons, dance displays, and bullfights.

The tranquil Río Oja, a tributary of the Ebro, runs along the western border of La Rioja, the region to which it gave its name.

Their faces tanned by outdoor working, three vine-growers gather in the village of Pesquera, in the south of the Rioja region.

Under the watchful eyes of prizewinning bulls, customers relax in a Madrid bar, famous for its tapas. A blood sport with ancient origins, bullfighting still flourishes in Spain.

Madrid's 18th-century Palacio Real, or Royal Palace, was built by Philip V on the site of the city's old Moorish fortress, which burnt down in 1734.

Castile-La Mancha and Madrid

The high, brown plateau of the Meseta is a romantic land still haunted by the spirit of Don Quixote. Cervantes' knight-errant and his servant Sancho Panza shared their adventures in a 17th-century landscape much like that of today. Fields of grain stretch as far as the eye can see; vines and thousands of acres of lavender and purple-flowering saffron cover the plains; avenues of almond trees lead to scattered, clay-colored villages. The idealistic knight famously jousted with the dazzling white windmills that still dot the landscape.

The fall saffron harvest – Spain produces 70 percent of the world's supply of this most highly prized spice, which until recently cost more per pound than gold – is celebrated by the election of a Saffron Queen, named for the lady of Don Quixote's dreams, Dulcinea de la Mancha. The historic towns and buildings of the region – Aranjuez, the royal summer residence; aristocratic Toledo; the monumental palace of El Escorial – recall the same age of chivalry.

Madrid, in contrast, is a relatively modern city. When it became Spain's capital in the 16th century it was a small provincial town; only within the last 200 years has it reached anything like its present size. It is a sprawling and vibrant capital – the highest in Europe – whose streets and squares bustle with life until late at night. The Madrileños, as the inhabitants are called, are renowned for an easy-going lifestyle. It is said that the city has more than 8,000 bars, most of them full at all hours of the day and night!

The contrast of countryside and city is reflected in the cuisine. Madrid is also Spain's gastronomic capital, a melting pot in which all the regional cuisines are available. The city stands amid virtual desert, and produce from all over the country is transported to its markets early every morning. The range of food available is remarkable, whether in the most expensive restaurants or the tiniest bars. Madrid is one of the few places in the heart of Spain where fresh seafood is common. During the early evening, customers enjoying tapas scatter their shrimp shells over the floor of the bar.

The main meal in the capital is traditionally eaten at lunchtime. It might begin with a salad or *Sopa de ajo* (garlic soup) and continue with a meat or fish entrée; or it might be a *Cocido madrileño*, the capital's version of a traditional Spanish dish. This slow-simmering casserole of meats, sausage, garbanzo beans (chickpeas), and vegetables is eaten in separate courses – first the broth, then the meat, and finally the vegetables.

The food of La Mancha is substantial rather than sophisticated, and based on

the ingredients to hand. This area is known as the *tierra de pan* – the land of bread – because of its vast grain fields. The typically large, flat loaves are eaten with such dishes as *Pisto manchego*, a vegetable stew traditionally made with fat pork. Toledo is renowned for its partridges; the bird may be served spiced with cinnamon and cloves or marinated in a mixture of seasonings and served cold. The city is also famous for its marzipan.

There is a range of other specialties. The sheep of the central plains yield the milk that goes to make the tangy queso manchego, the most popular of all Spanish cheeses. Stamped with a flower as a mark of quality, it is also characterized by the corded pattern left on the rind by the hemp string that binds the cheese as it matures.

The plains of La Mancha are one of the largest wine-producing areas of Spain, but the wine, like the food, tends to be robust. In recent years, though, some superior wines have emerged. The town of Valdepeñas gives its name to mainly soft reds, which are drunk as everyday table wines throughout Spain.

Festivals

For two weeks in May, Madrid stages a huge fiesta of fireworks, bullfights, and concerts in honor of San Isidro Labrador, the city's patron saint. In contrast, Toledo marks Corpus Christi with a solemn procession.

Symbols of peace and war, whitewashed windmills and a ruined 12th-century castle stand on a hilltop above the little town of Consuegra. The windmills, part of a group of seven, are still used throughout the region to grind grain.

Toledo's spires are reminiscent of the works of one of its most famous citizens, the 16th-century painter El Greco. Spain's ancient capital has been declared a national monument, a testimony to its beauty and glittering past.

The monastery of Guadalupe is home to a "miraculous" image of the Virgin Mary, reputedly carved by St. Luke. Founded in 1340 by King Alfonso XI in gratitude for a victory over the Moors, the monastery became a center of learning and pilgrimage, and grew rich on tributes from the conquistadors.

Extremadura

The people of Extremadura call their region "Land of the conquistadors, land of the gods." As many as one-third of the conquerors of the New World hailed from Extremadura, including Hernán Cortés, colonizer of Mexico, and Francisco Pizarro who conquered Peru. Those who returned built the ornate palaces that dignify many Extremaduran towns. But this proud history had its roots in poverty and emigration. The dry plains and hills of this vast, arid region, which is cut off from the rest of Spain by high sierras to the north and south, and the frontiers of Portugal to the west, have long been unable to feed its population. The name itself comes from the Latin terra extrema et dura – harsh, extreme land. Even today, the province remains sparsely populated and unvisited.

Many of those who do visit head for Guadalupe, a center of pilgrimage since the 14th century. The Virgin of Guadalupe, a small, black-faced cedar statue, was reputedly carved by St. Luke. The conquistadors carried the fame of "the patron of all Spanish lands" throughout the New World.

Religion figures prominently in Extremaduran history and, more surprisingly, its cuisine. Its isolated monasteries are centers of retreat. King Charles V lived in the monastery of Yuste, for example, for the year before his death in 1558, when he withdrew from the cares of this world to think about the next. In the monastic kitchens, which often provided hospitality for noble or royal guests, many outstanding recipes are said to have originated. One story claims that a cookbook smuggled out from one of them inspired French haute cuisine; another, that a French soldier, probably in Napoleon's army, declared that Extremaduran cooking made the invasion of Spain worthwhile.

Like other harsh lands, Extremadura depends on hardy animals and plants for its staples, and makes the most of little. Pigs forage among the cork oaks, pines, and sweet chestnut trees of the forests. Their meat is the source of delicate, air-dried hams such as that of Montánchez, near the regional capital Cjáceres. Morcón extremeño, a sausage famed throughout Spain, varies in flavor from slightly sweet to hot as chili; it comes in a range of shapes.

The forests constitute one of Spain's most important game reserves, yielding deer, hare, and game birds. "Take the sun from the hare and rabbit, and the shade from the partridge," says a hunter's proverb, referring to the animal's best meat: the saddle in one case, the breast in the other. The pheasant and partridge appear on local menus combined with truffles, another specialty: black winter truffles or *criadillas de tierra*, a pale, spotted truffle unique to Extremadura.

The cattle and sheep that graze on pastures bright with wild flowers provide meat for other dishes. When the animals move north to the cool mountains in the summer an eerie emptiness falls over the land. Wild thyme and eucalyptus scent the air; in the south, slender wild asparagus is common. Vegetables and fresh fruits The sun-soaked river valleys, the region's favorite dessert. grow in the lush river valleys.

Extremadura, though not a major wine-producing area, has some respectable table wines, including the refreshing white Almendralejo and the sherry-like whites from Cañamero, which are among the world's strongest unfortified wines. Of the reds, the robust Lar de Barros is an excellent choice.

Festivals

Every October, Guadalupe celebrates the discovery of America, because it was here that Columbus received the king's permission to set sail. Many Extremaduran pigs are dedicated to St. Anthony, and his feast-day in January is marked by a slaughter of mature hogs and the blessing of piglets, which are sprinkled with holy water.

Women dance in Trujillo's Plaza Mayor, one of Spain's finest squares. Though little more than a village in size, Trujillo is full of grandiose architecture, the legacy of the riches sent home by the conquistadors.

The Levante: Murcia and Valencia

To the Moors who settled here 1,200 years ago, the Levante was heaven on earth. Today, it still enjoys the blessings of a mild Mediterranean climate, plentiful sunshine, and rich soil. The Levante – the name means "land of the sunrise" or the East – is Spain's vegetable garden: the truck-farms of the plain around the city of Valencia can produce three or four vegetable harvests a year. This plenty is not entirely natural, however. To counter low rainfall, the Romans built irrigation canals, which were later improved by the Moors.

Moorish influence is also visible in the Arabian appearance of the villages scattered along the Costa Blanca, or white coast, named for the color of its sand. To the north lies the Costa del Ahazar, the orange blossom coast; here, in the evenings, the white blossom fills the air with its fragrance.

The regions is Spain's *zona de los arroces* – land of the rice. The emerald-green paddies around the Albufera lagoon produce rice for many regional dishes, including the Levante's best-known dish and the most famous in Spain: paella. *Paella valenciana*, the local version, can vary enormously. At its simplest it consists of rice and a little fish, betraying its origins as a dish of the poor; the most lavish version, on the other hand, contains many different kinds of meats, fish, and vegetables, luxuriously garnished with crawfish. Whatever the ingredients, *paella* should be cooked in and eaten from the two-handled pan after which it is named; traditionally it is eaten only at lunch-

time, no doubt because it is so rich.

The variety of fish and shellfish is not used only for paella. There are fresh anchovies, also served as tapas marinated in vinegar, the popular *Boquerones en vinagre*, and gray mullet, whose roe is as expensive and exquisite as caviar. Lake Albufeira, famous for its eels, also lends its name to a garlic-and-almond sauce eaten with fish. It was the Moors who introduced almond trees to the region; they are used as the basis for marzipan and various candies, desserts, and pastries. The most famous, *turrón*, is a nougat made in Alicante from toasted almonds, honey, and egg whites.

The most important legacy of the invaders, however, remains the irrigated market gardens of Valencia, called huertas. They provide bell peppers, tomatoes, onions, artichokes, and asparagus, best tasted in the fresh, crisp *ensalada mixta* that accompanies most meals in the region. In Murcia, the Moorish influence is evident in dishes of sweet roasted peppers and tomatoes. Another local specialty is *tronchón*, a

The paddy fields of the Levant lie where the hills meet the coastal plain just south of Valencia. Almost all of Spain's rice is grown here.

creamy ewe's milk cheese made in rounds with a funnel-shaped hollow on the sides.

Citrus and pomegranate trees line the roads and canals, and vines all-purpose flourish in the sun. The Levante is one of Spain's major producers of table wines. Vineyards are concentrated largely around Valencia, where Utiel-Requeña and Alicante, the region's best wines, are made. Perhaps the most characteristic drink, however, is *sangría*, Spain's famous punch of red wine and citrus fruits, which captures the Levante's sunny character.

Festivals

In mid-May, Valencia is the setting for a carnival called Fallas, a local word meaning "fire." Huge, papier-mâché figures decorate the town's squares for a week, then are burned on enormous bonfires. Alicante holds a smaller, similar festival called Fogueras on June 24. In late April, the citizens of Alcoy re-enact a historic battle for the Festival of Moors and Christians, which ends with the Moors being driven from the town.

In Caravaca, Murcia, men in magnificent costumes gather for the annual re-enactment of a battle between the Moors and Christians. Such ceremonies are also held in many other parts of the country.

The heavily ornamented façade of Murcia's 18th-century cathedral is one of Spain's outstanding examples of baroque architecture. The wealth of carvings represent scenes from paradise and the figures of the saints.

Picked out on its hilltop against a background of snow-capped peaks, Granada's Alhambra, or "Red Fort," glows in the evening sun. The exotic and splendid fortified palace remains Spain's finest example of Moorish artistry.

Andalucía

Andalucía is what most people imagine when they think of Spain – blazing sun, whitewashed villages, and Moorish castles, the land of Carmen and of flamenco music performed by sloe-eyed gypsies. But this view, shared by the thousands of tourists who flock to the sun-drenched beaches of the Costa del Sol, is far too simplified. Andalucía hides many contrasts.

West of the Costa del Sol lies the Costa de la Luz, the Coast of Light, as unspoiled as its neighbor is developed; the Coto Coñana National Park is one of Europe's richest nature reserves. The icy ramparts of the Sierra Nevada lie only a few hours from the golden beaches. And while flamenco seems to typify the fiery Spanish character, Andalucía's Arabian architecture, its apricots and almonds, even its predilection for barbecues and cookouts, are reminiscent of North Africa. The famed Alhambra

in Granada and the Mosque of Córdoba testify to the grandeur of the Moorish rule that lasted for over 700 years here.

Andalucían cookery and lifestyle reflect a climate that is itself more African than European. Western Europe's highest-ever recorded temperature, 138.6 degrees (45°C) was recorded in the Guadalquivir Valley. Local dishes match the weather; easy to prepare and easily digestible, they range from fried fish to gazpacho, a cold vegetable soup based on tomatoes, garlic, and bread which has become a classic of international summer cuisine.

In the hottest months, Andalucíans often go without a proper meal. As a local saying observes, "In Seville people don't eat meals, they nibble tapas." Bars offer these appetizers in such abundance that they fill both the evening and the stomach. There are Spanish olives, mostly produced in Andalucía; whitebait and shrimp, deep-fried and served in little bowls with a spicy sauce; different types of cold meats and sausages; crispy potato balls; mushrooms and vegetables served in a variety of marinades. Other local delicacies include hard, air-dried hams from Jabugo and Trevélez, and *huevos a la flamenca*, eggs sautéed in olive oil and garnished with vegetables from the fertile plains of Granada. As in the Levant, confectionery is based on almonds, pine nuts, honey, cinnamon, and eggs: yemas, or candied egg yolks, are particularly popular.

The glory of Andalucía, however, is sherry, a blend of wines fortified with spirits such as brandy. Sherry is the traditional accompaniment to tapas: the word *tapa* means literally a "lid" and originally referred to a little piece of bread, placed on top of the sherry glass to keep the flies off. Traditionally, between tapas you sip a dry light fino with a delicate almond flavor. Sweeter sherries go better with dessert.

Sherry derives its name from the town of Jerez de la Frontera, and although many countries produce sherry-like wines, only sherry from Jerez is authentic. The finest and most famous sherry producers still have their head-quarters in the town. In the massive bodegas or storehouses, large oak casks or barrels, are stored in rows stacked up to five layers high while the sherry matures to achieve its optimum flavor.

There are four basic types: fino is dry and pale; amontillado is darker in color and a little sweeter; oloroso, which means "fragrant," is a deep amber and accompanies desserts; while cream sherry, thicker and syrupy, is the sweetest of all. The Spanish, however, prefer their sherry dry.

One of the prettiest of Andalucía's famed white towns, Vejer de la Frontera perches on a rocky crag above the Costa de la Luz. The town's quaint beauty belies its former role as a border stronghold during the occupation of Granada by the Moors.

Festivals

Andalucía is rich in festivals marking its distinctive character. Each September, Jerez celebrates the grape harvest; in April or May, it stages a horse show. Córdoba hosts a flamenco festival in May, while Pentecost sees a gypsy pilgrimage to El Rocío. At the end of June, a music and dance festival takes place in Granada. Some of the most spectacular festivals, however, occur in Seville, which not only stages a Feria, or folklore festival in April, but is also the site of Spain's most elaborate celebration of Holy Week.

Little girls in traditional Andalucían costume celebrate the annual spring festival at Niebla, west of Seville.

The Balearic and Canary Islands

Spain's island groups – the Balearics in the Mediterranean and the Canaries in the Atlantic off North Africa – both suffered for many years from their popularity as vacation destinations. Concrete monstrosities threatened their picturesque coasts, while a tide of fast food swamped their respective cuisines. Yet the damage has now been largely halted: the islands have recaptured some of their original beauty, and local restaurants are returning more and more to traditional regional foods.

The cuisine of the island of Majorca, the largest of the Balearics – the others are Minorca, Ibiza, and tiny Formentera – is dominated by pork, sausages, figs, and almonds. The flavorings and seasonings of the more sophisticated dishes often reveal strong Moorish influences, as does the frequent combination of meat and fruit: turkey with almonds, for example, chicken served with pomegranates and pork, or veal with figs, almonds, and raisins.

As in those parts of the mainland that fell under Moorish sway, almonds are the basis of many desserts and candies, from almond milk to almond ice cream. Another delicacy comes from the old town of Palma, the regional capital, in which historic bakers' ovens called *fornos* are to be found on many street-corners These are used to bake *ensaimadas*, fat spirals of sweet yeast dough, which range in size from a small breakfast version to enormous "wagon wheels." Fresh fruit is provided by the citrus plantations of Sóller, on the island's northern coast.

The three smaller islands are less agricultural than Majorca, and their cooking is dominated by fish from the waters of the Mediterranean. Mussels and other shellfish are often added to traditional fish soups. Minorca, however, also produces its own cheese, hard tangy queso de Mahón, which resembles Parmesan.

Good red and white wines come from the cellars of Binisalem and Felanitx on Majorca. There are also a number of

Young women in traditional costume join in the annual Festival of the Brave Women, celebrated every May in Sóller on Majorca.

The white paint and palm trees are typical of the harbor of Puerto de Móga, a fishing village in the extreme south of Gran Canaria. The Romans reputedly named the island for its large number of dogs, canes in Spanish.

interesting digestifs, liqueurs made from herbs, leaves, flowers, or citrus fruits.

The Canary Islands are ten times closer to Morocco than they are to Spain, and their landscapes have a North African character of arid deserts, planted with cactus and succulents on their southern exposure and lush tropical plant cover elsewhere.

The islands' cuisine demonstrates the influence not only of the Moors, but also of Africa and even South America. Gofio, a cornbread which dates back to the Canaries' original inhabitants, the Guanches, is often served in place of bread. Another popular dish is a characteristic sauce called *mojo*, which is often used as a dip: mild *mojo verde* is made with lots of parsley, cilantro, and cumin, while a hot version, *mojo picón*, contains paprika, chili pepper, and garlic.

Canary Island desserts tend to be oriental in flavor and sickly-sweet, but the islands are major fruit growers and there is an especially plentiful supply of bananas, prickly pears (cactus fruits), and refreshing nísperos (loquats.)

The best Canary wine comes from the islands of Hierro and Lanzarote. The heavy sweet or dry Malmsey from Tenerife is drunk diluted, as a refresher or aperitif.

Festivals

Majorca has a number of major celebrations. In early May, a re-enacted battle marks the Festival of the Brave Women, which commemorates a 15th-century incident when the women of Sóller saved their town from attack by pirates. The island's capital, Palma, hosts an annual culinary fair each May at which many delicious foods can be sampled. And in September, the Vilafranca de Bonany is home to a melon festival.

Past glories and present pleasures meet in the Canary Islands. Now relatively unimposing, Betancuría on Fuerteventura (top) was once the island's capital and royal city. At a seafront restaurant in Arrieta in the north of Lanzarote (above) diners enjoy fresh fish served with sweet potatoes.

TAPAS

For most Spaniards, the working day ends with an aperitivo, enjoyed at home or, more often than not, at a local bar in the company of friends or colleagues. This uniquely Spanish way of sharpening the appetite traditionally consists of a glass of chilled fino or manzanilla sherry, accompanied by an array of little snacks known as tapas. The name derives from the original practice of using a piece of bread as a lid (tapa) to keep flies off the wine. A popular social pastime is to visit a number of bars throughout the evening, eating a selection of different tapas at each, in place of a full-blown dinner.

Tapas, which are also eaten before the midday meal, are endlessly varied. They range from such simple delights as salted almonds, stuffed olives, smoked serrano ham, or Manchego cheese, to more substantial hot or cold dishes such as kidneys with sherry, fried or marinated anchovies, deep-fried calamari rings, and the famous Spanish tortilla, a potato omelet.

Such is the variety and versatility of these appetizers that they are also becoming increasingly popular outside Spain. Because they are easy to prepare in advance as well as delicious to eat, they are a simple and inexpensive way of entertaining, and offer something to suit every taste.

Albóndigas en salsa de tomate

Needs a little time • Many regions   **Meat balls in Tomato Sauce**   *Serves 6*

1 large onion
6 tbsp. olive oil
1 tsp. dry (fino) sherry
3 beesteak tomatoes
1 bay leaf
½ cup meat broth
1 ¼ cups ground beef
1 ¼ cups ground pork
2 garlic cloves
3 tbsp. chopped
flat-leaved parsley
2 eggs
3 tbsp. fresh bread crumbs
salt
freshly ground back pepper
hot paprika

Preparation time: 1 hour

670 cal. per serving
(6 servings)

1 Peel and finely chop the onion. Heat 2 tbsp. olive oil in a saucepan and sauté the chopped onion over low heat until soft. Add the sherry.

2 Plunge the tomatoes briefly in boiling water; skin and halve them and remove the seeds. Finely chop the flesh and add it to the pan, together with the bay leaf. Add the broth and return to a boil over low heat. Cover the pan and simmer for about 30 minutes.

3 While the sauce is cooking, put the ground beef and pork in a bowl. Peel the garlic, crush it, and add it to the meat. Reserve half the chopped parsley and add the remainder to the meat. Add the

eggs and the bread crumbs. Mix thoroughly and season well with salt, pepper, and paprika.

4 With wet hands, shape the mixture into walnut-sized balls. Heat the remaining oil in a large skillet and fry the meatballs over medium heat until brown all over. Remove and drain.

5 Season the tomato sauce with plenty of salt, pepper, and paprika. Place the cooked meatballs in the sauce, simmer with the remaining parsley, and serve with crusty white bread.

Cebolletas al vinagre de jerez

Simple • Andalucía   **Pearl Onions in Sherry Vinegar**   *Serves 4 to 6*

1 ¼ lb. pearl onions
(or shallots)
6 tbsp. olive oil
⅔ cup sherry vinegar
1 clove
1 dried chili pepper
1 sprig thyme
1 bay leaf
1 tsp. black peppercorns
1 tsp. salt
1 pinch sugar

Preparation time: 1 hour
(plus about 1 hour cooling time)

180 cal. per serving
(if serving 6)

1 Peel the onions but leave them whole. Heat the oil in a wide sauté pan and fry the onions over medium heat until golden.

2 Pour in the vinegar and 1 cup water. Add the clove, chili pepper, thyme, bay leaf, peppercorns, salt, and a pinch of sugar.

3 Cover the pan and simmer over medium heat for about 30 minutes. Remove from the heat and leave to stand until completely cool.

Note: Pearl onions cooked in this way are also delicious served with grilled or stewed meat or game. The characteristic taste and spicy acidity of sherry vinegar adds a distinctive flavor to sauces, meat dishes, vegetables and salads. It is available from all good supermarkets and delicatessens.

33

Pimientos en adobo

Simple • La Rioja   **Marinated Red Peppers**   *Serves 4*

**4 large sweet red peppers
(about 2 ¼ lb.)
4 garlic cloves
salt
freshly ground black pepper
hot paprika
¾ cup virgin olive oil
1 tbsp. sherry vinegar
Preparation time: 35 minutes
(plus at least 2 hours marinating time)
500 cal. per serving**

1 Light the broiler or preheat the oven to 475 degrees. Wash the peppers, wipe dry, and place under the broiler, turning at intervals, or in the oven for 10 to 12 minutes, until the skins are scorched and blistered. Place in a covered bowl or closed paper bag; the effect of the steam will make the peppers easier to peel. When they are cool enough to handle, peel the peppers using a paring knife.

2 Meanwhile, peel the garlic cloves and cut them into thin slices.

3 Cut the sweet peppers in half, remove the seeds and ribs, and cut the flesh into strips about 1 inch wide.

Place the strips in a bowl and season with salt, pepper, and paprika.

4 Scatter the sliced garlic over the peppers and sprinkle with the oil and the vinegar, making sure that the peppers are well coated in the marinade. Cover, and refrigerate for at least 2 hours.

Variation: In the Basque country, skinned strips of sweet pepper are briefly fried in oil, then seasoned with a dash of chili pepper, garlic, salt, and pepper.

Note: Marinated sweet peppers are also a delicious accompaniment to broiled meats.

Riñones al jerez

Not difficult • Andalucía   **Kidneys in Sherry**   *Serves 4 (or 2 as a entrée)*

**1 calf's kidney (about 1 lb.)
milk for soaking
1 medium onion
1 garlic clove
2 tbsp. virgin olive oil
¾ cup dry (fino) sherry
1 small bay leaf
salt
freshly ground black pepper

Preparation time: 35 minutes
(plus 30 minutes soaking time)

180 cal. per serving**

1 Cut the kidney in half lengthwise, peel off the surface membrane, and cut out the fatty core. Rinse the kidney and place it in a bowl. Add enough milk to cover and leave to soak for at least 30 minutes.

2 Meanwhile, peel and finely chop the onion. Peel the garlic.

3 Remove the kidney from the milk, pat dry, then cut into medium-thin slices. Heat the oil in a skillet and fry the slices, in batches if necessary, over high heat. Remove and set aside.

4 Add the chopped onion to the pan and sauté over medium heat until soft. Crush the garlic and add it to the pan. Add the sherry and the bay leaf, and simmer for about 3 minutes. Season the kidney slices with salt and pepper and return them, together with any juices, to the pan. Heat through for a further 3 minutes. Serve immediately, with fresh white bread.

Variation: Chicken livers can be substituted for the calf's kidney.

Croquetas de pollo

Chicken Croquettes

1 small chicken breast, boned and
skinned
(about 5 ½ oz.)
1 tbsp. virgin olive oil
1 garlic clove
salt
freshly ground white pepper
2 tbsp. butter
3 to 4 tbsp. all-purpose flour
1 cup milk
pinch of freshly ground nutmeg
5 tbsp. fresh bread crumbs
1 egg
oil for frying (see page 71)

**Preparation time: 50 minutes
(plus 30 minutes chilling time)**

240 cal. per croquette

1 Heat the 1 tbsp. olive oil in a skillet and fry the chicken for about 10 minutes over medium heat, until lightly browned. Meanwhile, peel and crush the garlic, sprinkle it over the chicken, and season with salt and pepper. Remove the chicken from the pan and set it aside to cool.

2 Melt the butter over low heat in a saucepan. Add 2 tbsp. of the flour and, stirring, cook for about 2 minutes. Slowly pour in the milk, blending with a whisk to prevent lumps from forming. Whisking continuously, cook for a further 6–8 minutes, or until the sauce thickens. Remove from the heat.

3 Using a food processor, grind the chicken very finely, then stir it into the white sauce. Season generously with

salt, pepper, and nutmeg. Refrigerate for about 30 minutes.

4 With floured hands, shape the mixture into small croquettes. Put the remaining flour and the bread crumbs on separate shallow bowls. Whisk the egg and pour it into a third shallow bowl. Dip each croquette first in the all-purpose flour, then in the beaten egg, and finally in the bread crumbs, rolling it so that it is completely coated.

5 Fill a deep-sided skillet with a generous amount of oil and deep-fry the croquettes for 3 to 4 minutes, until golden. Remove from the pan and drain on kitchen paper. Serve hot or cold.

Variation: The croquettes can also be made with ham, salt cod, or veal.

Ensalada de zanahoria

Carrot Salad

1 ¼ lb. carrots
2 garlic cloves
3 tbsp. white wine vinegar
4 tbsp. virgin olive oil
1 tsp. ground cumin
½ tsp. mild paprika
1 to 2 tsp. fresh chopped oregano
leaves, or ½ tsp. dried oregano
salt
freshly ground black pepper

**Preparation time: 35 minutes
(plus 4 to 12 hours marinating time)**

**86 cal. per serving
(if serving 6)**

1 Wash and peel the carrots. Put them in a saucepan, add just enough water to cover them, and bring it to a boil. Reduce the heat to medium, cover the pan, and cook for 10 to 15 minutes, or until tender.

2 Meanwhile, peel and mince the garlic. Combine it with the vinegar, olive oil, cumin, paprika, oregano, salt, and pepper.

3 Drain the carrots and cut them into slices ¼ inch thick. Stir the slices into the marinade and leave to marinate for at least 4 hours, preferably overnight.

Note: Carrot salad goes well with meat or poultry tapas and is also good served as a side dish with grills. Cumin, a spice native to the Mediterranean region, was introduced to Spain by the Moors. It is also widely cultivated in Asia and an ingredient in many curries and meat dishes. Similar in appearance to caraway seeds, it is available either whole or ground but should be used sparingly, as it has a pungent aroma and a strong, hot flavor.

Pipirrana

Simple • Mága **Summer Salad** *Serves 4 to 6*

1 small red bell pepper
1 small green bell pepper
1 small cucumber
1 small Spanish onion
2 beefsteak tomatoes (about 400 g)
4 tbsp. red wine vinegar
salt
freshly ground black pepper
5 tbsp. virgin olive oil
3 or 4 garlic cloves

Preparation time: 30 minutes
(plus 1 hour marinating time)

110 cal. per serving
(if serving 6)

1 Wash the peppers; cut them in half lengthwise and remove the stalk, seeds, and ribs. Peel the cucumber, cut it in half lengthwise and scrape out the seeds with a spoon. Peel the onion. Finely dice all three vegetables and place in a bowl.

2 Plunge the tomatoes briefly in boiling water, skin, halve, and remove the seeds. Dice the flesh and add it to the other vegetables.

3 Mix the vinegar with the salt, pepper, and olive oil. Peel the garlic cloves, crush them, and stir into the vinaigrette.

Pour the dressing over the vegetables and stir in thoroughly. Leave to marinate in the refrigerator for about 1 hour. Serve with white bread.

Variation: Salpicón de mariscos
(Shellfish Salad)
Prepare half the quantity of the above salad, then toss in cooked shellfish, such as jumbo shrimp, mussels, or scallops.

Note: Pipirrana is also an ideal accompaniment for meat or poultry.

Pinchos morunos

Not difficult • Córdoba

Moorish-style Kabobs

Serves 4 (or 2 as an entrée)

1 ½ lb. lean pork fillet
1 tsp. ground cumin
2 tbsp. mild paprika
5 tbsp. olive oil
salt
freshly ground black pepper
cayenne pepper
4 cherry tomatoes

Preparation time: 30 minutes
(plus 1 hour marinating time)

380 cal. per serving

1 Cut the pork fillet into little cubes about ¾ in square.

2 In a large bowl, combine the cumin, paprika, olive oil, a pinch each of salt and pepper and a little cayenne pepper. Add the meat cubes to the marinade, mix well, and refrigerate for about 1 hour.

3 Preheat the broiler. Thread the cubes of meat tightly onto small wooden skewers (about 20) and broil them for 10 to 12 minutes, turning frequently and basting with the marinade, until well browned. (Alternatively, they can be pan-fried over medium heat.) Cut the cherry tomatoes in half and use them to garnish the kabobs. Serve with white bread.

Variation: If serving this dish as an entrée, cut the meat into larger cubes and increase the cooking time slightly. Accompany it with mashed potatoes and a green vegetable or a mixed salad.

Note: These highly spiced kabobs were originally made with lamb. Such dishes date back to the Moorish occupation of Spain, when many new foods and seasonings were introduced, among them spices such as cumin.

Tortilla de gambas
Shrimp Omelet

Serves 4

Quick and easy • Many regions
½ lb. cooked, shelled shrimp
juice of ½ lemon
3 tbsp. olive oil
4 eggs
salt
freshly ground black pepper

Preparation time: 20 minutes

260 cal. per serving

1 Place the shrimp in a bowl and sprinkle them with the lemon juice.

2 Heat the olive oil in an 8-inch skillet and briefly toss the shrimp in the oil.

3 Whisk the eggs thoroughly with a little salt and pepper. Pour the beaten eggs over the shrimp in the pan and cook over low heat for about 5 minutes, until the omelet begins to set.

4 Remove the pan from the heat. Invert a plate over the pan and flip the omelet onto it. Carefully slide the omelet back into the pan and cook the other side for a further 5 minutes.

5 Cut the omelet into wedges or bite-sized cubes and serve, hot or cold, with fresh white bread.

Variations: Tortillas come with an endless variety of fillings and many can be served as tapas. For example, instead of the shrimp, finely dice 3 medium-size green bell peppers, 1 onion, and 1 skinned, deseeded beefsteak tomato, and sauté them in the oil until soft; then pour on the beaten egg and proceed as above. Or, for a spinach tortilla, mix 2 cups sautéed spinach leaves with a little garlic and 1 tbsp. toasted pine nuts.

Ensaladilla rusa
Russian Salad

Serves 4 to 6

Not difficult • Many regions

3 cups waxy new potatoes
2 cups green beans
salt
2 cups carrots
1 cup garden peas, freshly shelled, or frozen
freshly ground black pepper
4 tbsp. sherry vinegar
3 egg yolks (see Note)
1 tbsp. lemon juice
1 cup olive oil

Preparation time: 45 minutes
(plus 30 minutes chilling time)

520 cal. per serving
(if serving 6)

1 Wash the potatoes. Place in a pan, cover with water and bring to a boil. Cook until tender but still firm.

2 Meanwhile, trim and wash the green beans. Bring a pan of salted water to a boil, add the beans and cook for about 10 minutes. Peel and finely dice the carrots, put them, together with the fresh peas, in another pan of boiling salted water and cook for about 5 minutes (if using frozen peas, add them 1 to 2 minutes before end of cooking time.)

3 Drain all three vegetables, rinse in cold water, drain again thoroughly, and place in a mixing bowl.

4 Peel the potatoes and dice them into ¼ inch cubes. Add to the rest of the vegetables. Season the mixture with salt and pepper, and sprinkle with the sherry vinegar.

5 In another bowl, combine the egg yolks with the lemon juice, salt, and pepper. Whisking vigorously, add the olive oil very gradually, to make a creamy mayonnaise. Mix the dressing into the vegetables and refrigerate about 30 minutes.

Note: Use only very fresh eggs from a source you trust. Raw eggs may carry the salmonella bacteria that causes food poisoning.

Gambas al ajillo

Garlic Shrimp

Serves 4

1 ¼ lb. fresh raw shrimp
2 red chili peppers, fresh or dried
(see Glossary)
6 or 8 garlic cloves
¾ cup olive oil
salt
freshly ground black pepper

Preparation time: 20 minutes

570 cal. per serving

1 Shell and de-vein the shrimp. Rinse in cold water and pat dry.

2 Wash the chili peppers and halve them lengthwise. Remove the seeds and cut into thin rings. (If using dried chilies, crush them in a mortar.) Peel the garlic and quarter lengthwise.

3 Heat the olive oil in a skillet. Add the chilies, garlic, and shrimp. Lightly season with salt and pepper and cook over high heat for 2 to 3 minutes.

4 Serve immediately in small dishes, accompanied by fresh white bread.

Note: Garlic shrimp are one of the most popular tapas; they are often served in the same small pans or earthenware dishes in which they were cooked. Freshly cooked or frozen shrimp can be used instead of raw ones. If using cooked shrimp, heat them only very briefly; otherwise they will be tough. A good, mild-tasting olive oil is best for this dish.

Garlic

The bulbs of this aromatic and pungent plant, familiar since ancient times, are a classic ingredient of many national cuisines, notably those of the Mediterranean. One of the largest producers of garlic is Spain, where it is used in generous amounts in fish, meat, and poultry dishes, as well as in sausages, soups, and sauces.

Long celebrated for its nutritive and medicinal properties, research indicates that garlic promotes the circulation of blood to the brain.

Two basic types of Spanish garlic are available all year round: *ajo blanco*, the universal white garlic, and the more expensive *ajo morado* with a reddish-violet skin, which is exported in large quantities. The fresher the garlic, the better the flavor and the greater nutritional value. Always choose fresh, plump bulbs – they should be rock hard – and avoid those showing green shoots, as these can impart a bitter taste to food and are indigestible. Stored in a cool dry place, exposed to the air, garlic should keep for several months.

Pechuga de pollo en jerez

Chicken in Sherry

Quick and easy • Andalucía   *Serves 4*

*1 ½ lb. chicken breast,
skinned and boned
salt
all-purpose flour for coating
2 tbsp. olive oil
freshly ground black pepper
1 cup dry (fino) sherry
1/2 cup chicken broth
2 garlic cloves
1 sprig thyme
1 small jar (about 2 oz.) olives
stuffed with red pimientos*

Preparation time: 40 minutes

260 cal. per serving

1 Cut the chicken breast into strips 1 inch long, season with salt, and roll them in the flour to coat.

2 Heat the olive oil in a large skillet and briefly fry the chicken pieces over high heat until browned. Season with salt and pepper, remove from the pan, and set aside.

3 Pour off the remaining oil and return the pan to the heat. Add the sherry, then stir in the chicken broth. Peel the garlic cloves, crush them, and add to the pan. Break the sprig of thyme into small pieces and add to the sauce. Cook the sauce, uncovered, until reduced to about one third of its original volume.

4 Return the chicken pieces to the pan and simmer over low heat for about 10 minutes. Meanwhile, slice the stuffed olives, add them to the pan, and heat through. Serve immediately, with crusty white bread.

Champiñones rellenos

Not difficult • Extremadura

Stuffed mushrooms

Serves 4 to 6

16 to 20 large button mushrooms
1 small onion
2 tbsp. olive oil
10 oz. chorizos (see page 56)
1 garlic clove
salt
freshly ground black pepper
1 tsp. mild paprika
2 tbsp. chopped flat-leaved
parsley
tomatoes for garnish (optional)

Preparation time: 55 minutes

210 cal. per serving
(if serving 6)

1 Trim the mushrooms and rinse briefly or wipe with a cloth. Remove the stalks and chop finely. Set the caps aside.

2 Preheat the oven to 425 degrees. Peel and mince the onion. Heat half the olive oil in a skillet and sauté the onion over medium heat. Add the chopped mushroom stalks and continue to cook until most of the liquid has evaporated.

3 Skin the chorizos, or squeeze the sausagemeat straight from the skin into the pan. Stir it into the onion-and-mushroom mixture. Peel the garlic, crush the flesh, and add it to the pan. Fry over low heat for about 8 minutes.

4 Season the sausage mixture with salt, pepper, and paprika. Remove the pan from the heat and leave to cool a little, then stir in the chopped parsley.

5 Stuff each mushroom cap with a little of the sausage mixture. Grease a baking dish with the remaining oil and arrange the stuffed mushrooms side-by-side in the dish. Bake in the center of the oven for 10 to 12 minutes, or until the mushrooms begin to brown. Serve with white bread and, if you like, tomatoes cut into segments.

Boquerones en vinagre
Marinated Anchovies

1 ½ lb. fresh anchovies
substitute smelt or whitebait)
½ cup sherry vinegar
10 garlic cloves
small bunch flat-leaved parsley
(about 1 oz.)
salt
freshly ground black pepper
1 cup virgin olive oil

Preparation time: 25 minutes
(plus 2 ½ hours marinating time)

1,000 cal. per serving

1 To gut the fish, run your index finger or a knife along the belly. Gently pull the head free, then open the fish out flat and peel the head and backbone away from the flesh (*above*), pinching it loose at the tail. Wash thoroughly under cold running water and pat dry.

2 Press each fish flat into a "butterfly" shape and lay them in a shallow baking dish. Mix the sherry vinegar with 1 cup water and pour it over the fish (*above*). Leave to marinate for 1 to 1 ½ hours, until the flesh has whitened.

3 Meanwhile, peel and finely chop the garlic cloves – do not use a garlic press. Wash the parsley, shake dry, and chop coarsely.

4 Pour off the marinade and briefly rinse the fish under cold running water. Return them to the baking dish, season with salt and pepper, and sprinkle with the chopped garlic and parsley (*above*). Finally, pour the oil over the anchovies and leave them to marinate for a further hour, or until ready to use. Serve with crusty white bread.

Drink: Beer goes well with this dish.

Variation:
Deep-fried anchovies
Fried anchovies are also popular served as tapas. Leave the fish whole, season with salt and pepper, and coat with all-purpose flour. Deep-fry in olive oil until golden-brown and crisp. Serve hot, with lemon wedges.

Note: Marinated anchovies with baked potatoes make a delicious informal supper. Fresh anchovies are imported by good fish wholesalers but, if unavailable, smelts or whitebait (candlefish) are good alternatives.

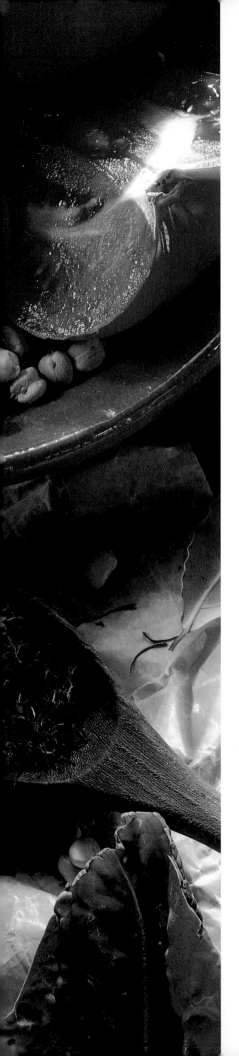

SOUPS AND STEWS

S panish soups and stews range from light first courses to complete one-pot meals. The latter are by far the more common. Soups are traditionally hearty and substantial, reflecting their origins as inexpensive but filling dishes for the poor. Pulses are the foundation of many delicious stews throughout Spain, and are a traditional part of meatless Lenten meals. But rich stews also depend on meat or fish, and every region has its own specialties which use the bounty of the surrounding land or sea. So distinctive are some of these recipes that they are almost bywords for local pride and tradition: the *cocidos* of Castile and Madrid, for example, made with boiled meats, sausages, and chickpeas, or the bean and sausage fabada of Asturias. The coastal regions offer marvelous fish and seafood stews such as the enowned *zarzuela* from Catalonia (see page 82).

Among the lighter soups is the garlic soup, *sopa de ajo*, which originally consisted only of water, bread, and garlic, but now appears in a range of more sophisticated forms. In the baking-hot climate of Andalucía, ice-cold gazpacho makes a refreshing first course. The standard version is tomato-based and red, but regional variations include a white type from Extremadura and a creamy, almond version from Málaga called *ajo blanco*.

Sopa de almendras

Fairly easy • Andalucía

Almond and Saffron Soup

Serves 4

¾ *cup shelled almonds*
5 garlic cloves
8 slices day-old white bread
small bunch flat-leaved parsley
(about 1 oz.)
5 tbsp. olive oil
salt
freshly ground black pepper
pinch of cumin
pinch of saffron
3 cups meat broth

Preparation time: 50 minutes

520 cal. per serving

1 Drop the almonds into boiling water and leave for 1 to 2 minutes, until the skins begin to loosen, then drain. Wrap in a towel and rub vigorously to remove the skins. Peel the garlic. Cut the bread into small dice. Wash and dry the parsley, discard the stalks, and reserve the leaves.

2 Heat the oil in a skillet and fry the bread, tossing frequently, until crisp and golden. Remove from the pan with a slotted spoon and reserve.

3 Add the almonds and garlic to the pan and cook over medium heat until they are golden. Add half the parsley and fry for about 3 minutes more. Grind in a food processor or vegetable mill, until smooth.

4 Transfer the purée to a heavy pan and season with salt, pepper, and a pinch each of cumin and saffron. Stir in the broth and slowly bring to a boil. Reduce the heat to low, cover the pan, and simmer for about 20 minutes.

5 Meanwhile, mince the rest of the parsley. When the soup is cooked, stir in half the fried bread and check the seasoning, as bread absorbs flavor. Serve hot, garnished with chopped parsley and the rest of the bread.

Saffron

The dried, orange-red stigmas of the saffron crocus have long been valued for their pungent flavor and exotic aroma, and for the brilliant yellow hue they give to food. Saffron was used by both Greeks and Romans, but it was the Arabs who introduced the spice to the Iberian peninsula, where is still features in many foods, particularly rice dishes.

Spain, where the purple saffron crocus flourishes, especially in the dry soil of Castile-La Mancha, produces two-thirds of the world's saffron supply – hence the spice's nickname, "Castillian Gold". Until recently, indeed, saffron cost more than gold and it is still the world's most expensive spice, retailing at about

$ 3750 a pound! The cost of saffron reflects the intensive labor required to produce it. Only the three stigmas from each flower are used, so it requires about 170 blooms to produce a single gram of spice. The plants flower overnight around mid-October, covering the fields with a carpet of purple. To preserve the flavor, they are picked by hand the same day, in hours of back-

breaking toil. The stigmas are then plucked from the flowers, spread on trays, and dried over charcoal fires.

Saffron is available in threads – the dried stigmas – or ground into powder; the threads generally have more flavor than the powder. It is sold in sachets, glass jars, or small metal cans. Because of its strong flavor, it is always used sparingly.

Soap de ajo

Not difficult · Castile

Garlic Soup

Serves 4

4 slices day-old white bread
1 head garlic
4 tbsp. olive oil
1 tsp. mild paprika
salt
freshly ground black pepper
4 cups meat broth
4 eggs

Preparation time: 1 hour

480 cal. per serving

1 Dice the bread in small cubes. Break the garlic into cloves and peel them.

2 In a skillet, heat the olive oil and fry the bread over medium heat, tossing frequently, until golden-brown. Crush the garlic cloves and add to the pan. Sprinkle with the paprika and season with salt and pepper. Pour in the broth, bring to a boil, then reduce the heat to low, cover, and simmer for about 20 minutes. Meanwhile, preheat the oven to 400 degrees.

3 Pour the soup into four individual ovenproof pottery bowls. Break the eggs carefully, one at a time, into a ladle or cup, and gently slide one into each bowl of soup.

4 Place the bowls in the center of the oven and bake for about 10 minutes, or until the eggs set. Serve immediately.

Note: Every region has its own version of garlic soup. Sometimes it is made with water, sometimes with broth, in some areas it might also contain tomatoes and bell peppers. One version in Cadiz, served sprinkled with shredded cheese, is known locally as Sopa de gato, or cat soup!

Cazuela de lentejas

Fairly easy · Catalonia

Lentil Casserole

Serves 4 to 6

1 head garlic
1 large onion
2 cloves
1 green bell pepper
1 ripe beefsteak tomato
3 tbsp. olive oil
1 tsp. mild paprika
hot paprika
cumin
1 ¼ lb. lentils
1 bay leaf
2 potatoes (about 1 lb.)
1 ¼ lb. chorizos (see page 56)
salt and freshly ground black pepper

Preparation time: 1 ½ hours

*880 cal. per serving
(if serving 6)*

1 Preheat the oven to 350 degrees. Place the whole garlic head on a rack or griddle and bake in the oven for about 15 minutes. Remove and leave to cool.

2 Meanwhile, peel the onion and spike it with the cloves. Wash the bell pepper and cut it in half. Remove the stalk, ribs, and seeds, and cut the flesh into strips. Plunge the tomato briefly into boiling water. Skin, halve, deseed, and coarsely chop the flesh. Carefully peel the baked garlic cloves and crush to a pulp.

3 Heat the oil in a large casserole or heavy saucepan. Briefly sauté the tomato and bell pepper, then stir in the mild paprika, a pinch of hot paprika, and a little cumin. Add the lentils, onion, bay leaf, and 3 cups water. Stir in the crushed garlic. Bring to a boil, cover the pan, and simmer over low heat for about 45 minutes, or until the lentils are tender.

4 Meanwhile, peel and wash the potatoes. Dice them finely and stir into the pan when the lentil mixture has been cooking for about 30 minutes. Add the chorizos in the last 5 minutes of lentil cooking time. Before serving, remove and discard the onion and bay leaf, and season the casserole with salt and freshly ground pepper. Serve hot with crusty white bread.

Wine: A strong red wine from Navarre or Rioja is especially good with this dish.

Purrusalda

Salt cod stew

1 ¼ lb. dried salt cod
6 leeks
2 garlic cloves
1 ¼ lb. potatoes
5 tbsp. olive oil
1 bay leaf
salt
freshly ground black pepper
1 tsp. mild paprika

Preparation time: 1 ¼ hours
(plus at least 24 hours soaking
time)

670 cal. per serving

1 Soak the salt cod in cold water for at least 24 hours, changing the water three or four times. The fish is ready for cooking when it has roughly doubled in size.

2 Remove the cod from the water, rinse, and reserve. Trim and wash the leeks, and slice into thin rings. Peel the garlic cloves and halve lengthwise. Peel and wash the potatoes and cut into ¼ inch slices.

3 Heat the olive oil in a flameproof casserole or heavy saucepan. Add the garlic and sauté over medium heat, stirring constantly, until golden. Remove from the pan with a slotted spoon and set aside. Add the leeks to the remaining oil and sauté until soft.

4 Stir in the potatoes, add the bay leaf, and season with a little salt and plenty of pepper. Add 3 cups water, bring to a boil, cover, and simmer over low heat for about 30 minutes.

5 Meanwhile, crush the fried garlic with a pestle and mortar or mash with a fork. Mix with the paprika and stir into the simmering vegetables.

6 Cut the fish into bite-sized pieces and add to the saucepan. Cook for about another 5 minutes, or until the fish is cooked and flakes easily. Serve with crusty white bread.

Note: Salt cod is available from gourmet and ethnic food stores.

Caldo de pescado

Easy • Canary Islands **Fish Soup**   *Serves 4*

2 large onions
2 ripe beefsteak tomatoes
6 red bell peppers
3 tbsp. olive oil
3 tsp. mild paprika
3 large garlic cloves
salt
1 tsp. coarsely crushed black pepper
1 tsp. cumin
1 ½ lb. firm-fleshed, white fish fillets
(for example, cod,
red snapper, or grouper)
2 tbsp. lemon juice

Preparation time: 50 minutes

240 cal. per serving

1 Peel and mince the onions. Plunge the tomatoes briefly into boiling water. Skin, halve, and deseed them, and coarsely chop the flesh. Wash the red bell peppers and cut them in half. Remove the stalks, ribs, and seeds and cut the flesh into small dice.

2 In a large saucepan or flameproof casserole, heat the olive oil and sauté the onions over low heat until transparent. Add the tomatoes and the paprika, and stir in thoroughly. Cook over low heat for a further 5 minutes.

3 Peel the garlic and crush directly into the pan. Season with a little salt, half the pepper, and the cumin.

4 Stir a third of the diced red peppers into the pan. Add 3 cups water, bring to a boil, reduce the heat to low, and simmer for about 20 minutes.

5 Meanwhile, rinse the fish under cold water, cut into bite-sized pieces, and sprinkle with the lemon juice. Season with salt and the remaining pepper.

6 Purée the soup in a food processor or vegetable mill, and return to the pan. Add the fish and remaining peppers to the puréed soup and bring to a boil. Cover the pan and simmer for about 5 minutes. Serve with crusty bread.

Callos a la gallega

Takes a little time • Galicia   Stewed Tripe with Chorizo   *Served 6 to 8*

1 ¼ cups dried chickpeas
3 cups cooked tripe (menudo)
2 tbsp. vinegar
2 onions
6 garlic cloves
3 ripe beefsteak tomatoes
5 oz. serrano ham
(or prosciutto if unavailable)
4 tbsp. olive oil
2 tsp. fresh, or 1 tsp. dried, thyme
salt • freshly ground black pepper
1 small, dried chili pepper (see Glossary)
1 bay leaf
3 cups meat broth
10 oz. chorizos (see below)
1 small bunch flat-leaved parsley (about 1 oz.)

Preparation time: 2 ¾ hours (plus soaking time)

430 cal. per serving (if serving 8)

1 Soak the chickpeas overnight in cold water.

2 The next day, cover the tripe with cold water, add the vinegar, and soak for about 30 minutes.

3 Meanwhile, peel and mince the onions and garlic. Plunge the tomatoes into boiling water, skin and deseed them, and coarsely chop the flesh. Finely dice the ham.

4 In a large saucepan, heat the olive oil and sauté the onions, garlic, and ham over low heat until the onions are transparent. Meanwhile, drain the tripe, cut it into thin strips, and add to the pan.

5 Stir in the tomatoes, and season with the thyme and some salt and pepper. Crush the chili pepper slightly with the back of a spoon and add to the pan with the bay leaf. Drain the chickpeas and stir into the pan. Add the broth, bring to a boil, cover, and simmer over low heat for about 2 hours.

6 Slice the chorizos and add to the saucepan about 15 minutes before the end of the cooking time. Meanwhile, wash the parsley, shake dry, remove the stalks, and mince the leaves. Remove the bay leaf from the stew and check the seasoning. Sprinkle with the minced parsley and serve with crusty white bread.

Chorizo

Chorizo, a red paprika sausage, is one of the most common and distinctive ingredients of Spanish cooking. It can be sliced and eaten cold as an appetizer, served broiled, or added to substantial and warming stews such as *Fabada asturiana* (page 61).

Each region has its own local version, with variations on the basic ingredients of salt pork and pork fillet, heavily flavored with garlic and paprika. In León and Galicia, for example, chorizo is lightly smoked; in Pamplona in Navarre it contains beef, as well as a generous quantity of paprika and a pinch of sugar, but little garlic; in Salamanca, regarded by connoisseurs as Spain's chorizo capital, sherry adds extra richness to the sausage mixture. There is even a very garlicky variation that contains no paprika, called *chorizo blanco*.

Whatever the variety, chorizo is available smoked or air-dried. If real Spanish chorizo is unavailable, Mexican chorizo is similar.

Ajo Blanco con Uvas

Chilled grape and almond soup

Not difficult • Málaga

Serves 4

*3 slices white bread
(about 3 oz.)*
½ cup almonds
3 garlic cloves
4 tbsp. olive oil
1 tbsp. white wine vinegar
salt • freshly ground white pepper
*⅔ cup seedless white grapes,
preferably muscatel*

Preparation time: 20 minutes

(plus 1 hour chilling time)
360 cal. per serving

1 Cut the crusts off the bread and discard. Soak the bread in cold water for about 10 minutes. Meanwhile, blanch the almonds (page 50, Step 1) and peel the garlic.

2 Squeeze as much moisture as possible from the bread, and purée with the garlic and almonds in a food processor or vegetable mill.

3 Place the purée in a large bowl and stir in the olive oil and 3 cups water.

Add the white wine vinegar and season with plenty of salt and pepper. Cover the bowl and place in the refrigerator to chill for at least 1 hour.

4 Meanwhile, peel and halve the grapes, and remove the seeds.

5 Before serving, stir the soup thoroughly and check for seasoning. Serve in individual bowls, sprinkled with the grapes.

Gazpacho

Cold vegetable soup

Fairly easy • Andalucía

Serves 4

*4 slices white bread,
crusts removed*
7 tbsp. olive oil
4 garlic cloves
cumin
3 ripe beefsteak tomatoes
1 cucumber
1 green bell pepper
salt
2 tbsp. red wine vinegar

*Preparation time: 40 minutes
(plus at least 1 hour chilling time)*

430 cal. per serving

1 Reserve 1 slice of the bread. Tear the rest into pieces, place in a bowl, and sprinkle with the olive oil. Peel and crush the garlic and add to the bread. Sprinkle with a little cumin, stir thoroughly, and leave to stand for about 30 minutes.

2 Meanwhile, plunge the tomatoes briefly into boiling water, skin, halve, and deseed. Finely dice half of one tomato, place it in a small bowl, and reserve. Coarsely chop the rest of the tomatoes and place in a food processor.

3 Peel the cucumber; finely dice about one third of it, place in a small bowl and reserve. Coarsely chop the rest and add to the tomatoes in the food processor.

4 Wash the bell pepper and cut in half. Remove the stalk, ribs, and seeds; finely dice about one third of the flesh, place in a small bowl and reserve.

Coarsely chop the remainder, and place in the food processor with the tomatoes and cucumber. Add the soaked bread and garlic, and purée the mixture until it is smooth.

5 Rub the purée through a fine sieve into a large bowl. If you prefer a soup with a thinner consistency, add 1 cup water. Season with salt and stir in the wine vinegar. Place in the refrigerator, together with the small bowls of diced vegetables, and chill for at least 1 hour.

6 Cut the reserved bread into small dice and place in a serving bowl. Check the gazpacho for seasoning and serve accompanied by the bread and vegetable garnishes.

Note: On very hot days, ice cubes are often added to gazpacho. A food-mill can be used instead of the food processor.

Potaje de garbanzos

Not difficult • Catalonia   **Chickpea and Spinach Stew**   *Serves 4*

1 ¼ lb. dried chickpeas
2 onions
1 carrot
2 tbsp. olive oil
1 bay leaf
salt
4 cups meat broth
4 garlic cloves
2 beefsteak tomatoes (about 1 ¼ lb.)
3 cups leaf spinach
freshly ground black pepper
3 eggs

*Preparation time: 1 ¾ hours
(plus 12 hours soaking time)*

620 cal. per serving

1 Soak the chickpeas overnight in plenty of cold water.

2 Peel and finely chop the onions. Peel and slice the carrot. Heat the olive oil in a large saucepan and sauté the onions and carrot over low heat until the onions are transparent.

3 Drain the chickpeas and add to the pan together with the bay leaf. Season with salt, pour in the broth, and slowly bring to a boil. Peel and halve the garlic cloves and stir into the chickpeas. Cover, and cook over medium-low heat for about 50 minutes. Remove and discard the bay leaf.

4 Meanwhile, plunge the tomatoes briefly into boiling water; skin, halve, and deseed them, and coarsely chop the flesh. Wash, trim, and coarsely chop the spinach. Stir the tomatoes and spinach into the chickpeas. Season with plenty of salt and pepper and cook for a further 20 minutes.

5 Meanwhile, in another saucepan, boil the eggs until hard-cooked, about 10 minutes. Plunge into cold water to stop the cooking, shell, finely chop, and place in a serving bowl. Check the stew for seasoning, as chickpeas absorb a lot of the flavor. Serve in individual dishes, sprinkled with chopped egg and accompanied by crusty white bread.

Fabada asturiana
Bean and Sausage Stew

Takes a little time • Asturias

Serves 4

*1 ¼ lb. dried white beans
navy or Great Northern beans)
2 onions
4 garlic cloves
5 oz. bacon
5 oz. serrano ham (or prosciutto if
unavailable)
2 tbsp. olive oil
3 tbsp. tomato paste
1 tbsp. mild paprika • 1 bay leaf
salt • freshly ground black pepper
pinch of saffron
2 chorizos (about 10 oz.)
2 morcillas (about 10 oz.)
(see Note)*

*Preparation time: 2 ⅓ hours
(plus 12 hours soaking time)*

1,200 cal. per serving

1 Soak the white beans overnight in plenty of water.

2 Peel and mince the onions and garlic. Finely chop the bacon and ham. Heat the olive oil in a large saucepan or flameproof casserole and sauté the onions and garlic until the onions are transparent. Stir in the tomato paste and paprika.

3 Drain the beans and add to the pan. Add the bacon, ham, and bay leaf, and season with a little salt and pepper. Do not oversalt, the ham and sausages are both very salty. Add 1 ½ quarts water, bring to a boil, then reduce the heat to low. Cover and simmer for about 1 ½ hours. Skim off any scum that forms on the surface from time to time.

4 Season with a little more pepper and the saffron. Add the chorizos and the morcillas and cook for a further 30 minutes. Check the seasoning and adjust if necessary. Remove and discard the bay leaf. Serve with crusty white bread.

Wine: Valdeorras, a light, Asturian red wine, is a good choice with this dish.

Note: Fabada asturiana, the best-known of Spain's substantial bean stews, is just right for the cold winter evenings of the northwest. It can be prepared in advance and reheated. It can also be made with ingredients such as pig's ears, tails, and feet. Morcilla is a Spanish blood sausage. If unavailable substitute a mild smoked sausage such as Polish kielbasa.

RICE, EGGS, AND VEGETABLES

Spanish cuisine is characterized by its inventive use of the most humble of ingredients such as rice, vegetables, and eggs, all of which are in plentiful supply. The vast paddies of Valencia produce the distinctive round-grain, starchy rice that lends itself to countless rice dishes. These vary from region to region and may include fish or seafood, meat, vegetables, poultry or, as in the case of paella, a mixture of all of them. This gloriously colorful medley of saffron rice, mixed seafood, and vegetables – its name derives from the large pan in which it is traditionally cooked – is one of Spain's most celebrated creations.

Among the great delights of Spain are its busy vegetable markets, where the produce from many regions is displayed. Potatoes are a staple served with most entrées; however, fresh, unadorned vegetables are not generally a prominent feature of the country's cuisine. Instead, the Spanish prefer to stew or fry their vegetables, or combine them with other ingredients to make such dishes as *Huevos a la flamenca* – originally a gypsy dish – a delicious combination of mixed vegetables, ham, and eggs.

Eggs also combine with potatoes to make another much-loved classic, *Tortilla de patatas*, or potato omelet. This simple and hearty dish has become a particular favorite, suitable for any occasion from a simple picnic or supper to a party.

Paella

More complex • Valencia

Chicken and Seafood Rice

Serves 6

2 red bell peppers (about 300 g)
6 beefsteak tomatoes
1 large onion
5 garlic cloves
1 oven-ready chicken (about 2 ½ lb.)
8 oz. pork loin
2 cups small clams in shell
6 raw jumbo shrimp
8 tbsp. olive oil
salt
freshly ground black pepper
1 ¼ cups freshly shelled, or frozen,
peas
pinch of powdered saffron
1 tsp. mild paprika
1 bay leaf
5 cups meat broth
1 ¼ lb. Spanish round-grain rice or
Italian arborio rice • 1 lemon

Preparation time: 2 ¼ hours

900 cal. per serving

1 Heat the broiler or preheat the oven to 475 degrees. Wash the peppers, wipe dry, and remove the skins (page 34, top recipe, Step 1). Halve the skinned peppers, remove the seeds and ribs and cut into narrow strips. Reduce the oven temperature to 350 degrees.

2 Plunge the tomatoes briefly in boiling water, skin, halve, and deseed. Coarsely chop the flesh. Peel and finely chop the onion and garlic.

3 Divide the chicken into 12 pieces. Dice the pork. Scrub the clams under cold running water, removing the beards; discard any that remain open. Rinse the shrimp.

4 Heat the olive oil in a paella or roasting pan (see note on opposite page). Fry the chicken pieces over high heat until brown all over. Remove from the pan, season with salt and pepper, and keep warm. Repeat with the diced pork. Add the clams to the pan and fry until they open; remove from the pan, discarding any that remain closed and keep warm. Finally, fry the shrimp until they turn red, remove from the pan, and keep warm.

5 In the remaining fat, sauté the chopped onion and garlic over medium heat until transparent. Add the tomatoes and peas, and sauté for about 5 minutes. Stir in the saffron and the paprika, then season generously with salt and pepper. Add the bay leaf.

64

6 In a saucepan, bring the meat broth to a boil. Add the rice to the other ingredients in the paella pan. Stir in the boiling broth and simmer for about 25 minutes, until the rice has absorbed most of the liquid. Stir in the strips of red pepper. Check the seasoning and adjust if necessary.

7 Arrange the chicken pieces, pork, clams, and shrimp over the rice. Cover the pan with foil and cook in the center of the oven for a further 15 minutes. Serve straight from the pan, accompanied by wedges of lemon.

Note: Although paella can be made with long-grain rice, the dish's characteristic moist, sticky texture is best achieved by using Spanish rice or a plump, round-grain risotto rice, which should be cooked for a short a time as possible. When serving paella, it is a good idea to provide finger-bowls of warm water and slices of lemon, as well as plates for the discarded bones and shells.

A **paella pan** is a large, round, flat-bottomed pan with metal handles.

A good alternative is a large flameproof casserole, wok, or a deep skillet (with a removable handle, if you complete the cooking in the oven). In Spain, paellas are sometimes cooked on an open fire; the flames lick round the edges of the pan, ensuring that the contents are heated evenly. At home, if using a relatively small pan, it is better to finish cooking the paella of the oven (as in Step 7), not on top of the stove.

Arroz emperado

Rice with White Beans

Takes a little time • Catalonia

Serves 4

⅔ cup dried navy or Great Northern
beans
1 garlic head
3 cups meat broth
1 pinch powdered saffron
1 bay leaf
1 ¼ cups Spanish round-grain rice
or Italian arborio rice
1 large beef tomato
2 tbsp. olive oil
1 tsp. mild paprika
salt
freshly ground black pepper

**Preparation time: 1 ¼ hours
(plus 12 hours soaking time)**

430 cal. per serving

1 Soak the beans overnight in cold water. Next day, discard the water, place the beans in a pan with 1 quart fresh water, cover, and bring to a boil. Reduce the heat to low and simmer for about 1 hour, until tender.

2 Meanwhile, break off 4 garlic cloves from head and set aside. Place the rest of the head, unpeeled, in another pan together with the broth and bring to a boil. Add the saffron and the bay leaf. Reduce the heat to low, sprinkle in the rice, cover, and simmer for about 20 minutes, until the liquid is absorbed.

3 Plunge the tomato briefly into boiling water, skin, halve, and remove the seeds. Chop into small pieces.

4 Heat the oil in a large pan. Peel the reserved garlic cloves and crush them into the pan. Stir in the paprika and the tomato, and cook for about 5 minutes.

5 Remove the garlic head and bay leaf from the rice. Drain the beans. Add the beans and rice to the large pan. Season generously with salt and pepper, stir thoroughly and serve.

Variation: For a vegetarian entrée, use vegetable broth instead of meat broth. You can also sprinkle the cooked rice with Manchego cheese (see page 75) and brown it under the broiler.

Note: This dish makes a good accompaniment for meat or poultry.

Alcachofas fritas

Fried Artichokes

Not difficult • Navarre

Serves 4 to 6

3 lemons
12 small young artichokes
4 to 6 garlic cloves
6 tbsp. olive oil
salt
freshly ground black pepper

Preparation time: 30 minutes

**180 cal. per serving
(if serving 6)**

1 Fill a large bowl with water, and add the juice of one of the lemons.

2 With a sharp knife, cut off the artichoke stalks, leaving a short stump. Remove the tough outer leaves, so that the base is almost exposed, and trim off the tips of the remaining leaves.

3 Wash the artichokes under cold running water to remove any grit, cut them into quarters, and drop into the acidulated water.

4 Peel and thinly slice the garlic. Heat the oil in a large skillet over medium heat. Remove the artichoke quarters from the water, pat dry, and fry in the

hot oil for about 5 minutes. Add the garlic, season with salt and pepper, and continue cooking for a further 5 minutes, or until golden.

5 Serve hot, with the remaining lemons cut into wedges.

Note: Very young artichokes have been used in this recipe. If you use slightly older ones, you may need to remove the chokes. Because artichokes react chemically to metals, such as aluminum, and contact with air discolors their cut edges, use only stainless steel knives and nonreactive pans, and put trimmed artichokes in acidulated water or rub the cut edges with lemon juice.

Espinacas Sacromonte

Not difficult · Granada   **Spinach with Almonds and Raisins**   *Serves 4*

2½ lb. leaf spinach
½ cup almonds
2 slices day-old white bread
5 tbsp. olive oil
2 garlic cloves
2 tbsp. raisins
salt
freshly ground black pepper
pinch of saffron threads

Preparation time: 40 minutes

360 cal. per serving

1 Trim the spinach, removing the stalks. Wash and drain.

2 Blanch the almonds (see page 50, Step 1). Cut the bread into small cubes.

3 In a skillet, heat 1 tbsp. olive oil. Add the blanched almonds and toast until golden-brown. Remove from the pan and set aside. Pour in a further 2 tbsp. oil, and fry the bread cubes until crisp. While the bread is frying, peel and crush the garlic into the pan. Transfer the mixture to a mortar or food processor, and grind to a paste.

4 In a large, heavy pan, heat the remaining olive oil. Sauté the spinach and raisins for about 5 minutes, until the spinach wilts. Stir in the almond paste and season with salt, pepper, and a few saffron threads. Heat through and serve.

Variation: Sauté the spinach with chopped onions, lots of garlic, and diced serrano ham. Season with salt, pepper and nutmeg. Serve hot or cold.

Note: Serve as a side dish with meat, fish, or poultry. With rice, this dish makes a good vegetarian entrée.

Pisto manchego

Simple · La Mancha   **Vegetable ragout**   *Serves 4*

3 ripe beefsteak tomatoes
1 large onion
3 garlic cloves
2 green bell peppers
1 ¼ lb. zucchini
3 tbsp. olive oil
salt
freshly ground black pepper
Small bunch flat-leaved parsley
(about 1 oz.)

Preparation time: 1 hour

150 cal. per serving

1 Plunge the tomatoes briefly into boiling water, then skin, halve, and deseed them. Coarsely chop the flesh. Peel and finely chop the onion. Peel the garlic.

2 Wash the bell peppers. Cut into quarters, remove the seeds and ribs, and cut into strips about 3/4 inch wide. Trim and wash the zucchini. Halve or quarter them lengthwise, depending on their size, and cut into 3/4-inch lengths.

3 Heat the oil in a pan and sauté the onion until transparent. Crush the garlic cloves into the pan. Stir in the bell peppers and the zucchini and sauté briefly.

4 Stir in the tomatoes, and season with salt and pepper. Cook, uncovered, over low heat for about 25 minutes, until almost all the liquid has evaporated.

5 Meanwhile, wash the parsley and shake dry. Tear off the leaves and chop them finely. Shortly before the end of the cooking time, stir the chopped parsley into the vegetables. If there is still too much liquid, increase the heat for the last few minutes.

Note: This dish can be served hot or cold with fish, meat, or poultry, or as a vegetarian entrée. In small servings it also makes ideal tapas.

Escalivada
Baked Mixed Vegetables

6 tbsp. olive oil
2 potatoes (about 1 ¼ lb.)
2 medium-sized onions
2 red bell peppers
2 small eggplant
2 medium-sized beefsteak tomatoes
juice of ½ lemon
salt
freshly ground black pepper

Preparation time: about 1 ¼ hours

310 cal. per serving

1 Preheat the oven to 350 degrees. Grease a cookie sheet with 2 tbsp. olive oil.

2 Wash the potatoes, cut in half lengthwise, and lay on the baking sheet, cut side downward. Place in the oven.

3 Meanwhile, peel the onions and cut in half crosswise. Wash and halve the red peppers, remove the seeds and ribs, and cut into wide strips. Wash the eggplant and remove the stalks. Slice lengthwise, then cut into strips.

4 When the potatoes have been in the oven for 15 minutes, place the onions on the cookie sheet, cut side down. After another 5 minutes, add the peppers and eggplant, and sprinkle with a little of the remaining olive oil.

5 Wash the tomatoes and cut in half crosswise. When the peppers and eggplant have been in the oven for about 20 minutes, turn them over, and place the tomatoes on the cookie sheet, cut side down. Continue to roast all the vegetables for a further 20 minutes.

6 Mix the remaining olive oil with the lemon juice. Arrange the vegetables on a serving dish, sprinkle with the oil and lemon dressing, and season with salt and pepper. Serve warm or cold.

Wine: A dry white wine from Catalonia goes well with this dish.

Note: Escalivada can accompany meat, fish, or vegetables, and also makes an excellent vegetarian entrée.

Olives and Olive Oil

The olive, native to the Mediterranean, has been cultivated for its oil and as a food since at least 3000 B.C. Today, about 90 percent of the world's olive production is used to make oil, with the rest of the fruits – inedible when raw – being cured and treated for the table. Spain is the world's largest producer, and major exporter, of table olives – green (half-ripe) or black (ripe), whole or pitted, or stuffed with almonds, anchovies, onions, pimientos, jalapeños, or capers.

Olives are still often painstakingly picked by hand. They are then sorted, washed, and processed as quickly as possible. At the oil-mill, the fruit is first crushed, then pressed, then placed in centrifuges to separate the oil from the olive juices. It takes 8¾ to 11 lb. of ripe fruit to produce one quart of oil.

The best quality oils come from the first cold pressings, and fall into two categories: unrefined extra virgin olive oil and virgin olive oil. Both have a rich, full flavor best suited to cold dishes and sauces, but not for frying. The oil from further, heated pressings is refined, blended and sold as pure, extra-fine or fine olive oil. These oils have less flavor and are more suitable for frying. In the Mediterranean Basin, olive oil is used for most cooking, even for deep-frying.

Berenjenas Alpujarra

Eggplant Alpujarra-style   *Serves 4*

**4 medium-sized eggplants
(about 3 lb.)
juice of ½ lemon
2 onions
2 ½ tbsp. olive oil
1 tbsp. chopped fresh mint
3 eggs
2 tbsp. fresh bread crumbs
4 tbsp. freshly grated Manchego
cheese (see page 75)
salt
freshly ground black pepper
large pinch of ground cinnamon

Preparation time: 1 hour

240 cal. per serving**

1 Preheat the oven to 350 degrees. Put the lemon juice in a large pan of water and bring it to a boil. Wash the eggplant, cut them in half lengthwise, and add them to the pan. Reduce the heat and simmer for about 5 minutes.

2 Using a sharp knife, remove most of the flesh from the eggplant (*above*), leaving a shell about ¾ inch thick. Chop the flesh into small cubes. Pare a little of the skin and flesh from the underside of each eggplant shell, so that they do not tip over when stuffed.

3 Peel and mince the onions. Heat 2 tbsp. of the oil in a skillet and sauté the onions until soft. Add the chopped eggplant flesh to the pan and cook for a further 10 minutes. Transfer to a bowl and leave to cool.

4 Wash the mint and shake dry. Tear off the leaves, chop them finely, and add to the onion-and-eggplant mixture. Add the eggs, bread crumbs, and 3 tbsp. of the grated Manchego cheese, and stir thoroughly. Season with plenty of salt, pepper, and ground cinnamon.

5 Grease an ovenproof dish with the remaining oil and arrange the eggplant cases in a single layer in the dish. Divide the mixture between the cases (*above*), then sprinkle with the rest of the cheese. Bake in the center of the oven for 15 to 20 minutes, until golden-brown. Serve with salad.

Wine: A light rosé from Navarre goes particularly well with this dish.

Variation: For the filling, instead of the eggplant flesh you could use 1 ½ lb. ground meat, which you would sauté with the onions (Step 3). The chopped eggplant flesh can then be stewed with 2 skinned, chopped beefsteak tomatoes, and the mixture puréed and served as a sauce.

Calabacines al horno

Not difficult · Murcia

Baked zucchini

Serves 4

1 large onion
3 garlic cloves
5 ½ tbsp. olive oil
1 lb. 5 oz. beefsteak tomatoes
salt
freshly ground black pepper
1 tsp. mild paprika
fresh thyme
2 ¼ lb. zucchini
all-purpose flour for coating
¾ cup freshly grated Manchego cheese

Preparation time: 1 hour

260 cal. per serving

1 Peel and finely chop the onion and the garlic. Heat 2 tbsp. of the oil in a skillet over medium heat, and sauté the onion and garlic until soft.

2 Meanwhile, plunge the tomatoes briefly into boiling water, skin, halve, and deseed. Chop the flesh and add it to the skillet. Season with salt, pepper, the paprika, and thyme leaves. Continue to cook, uncovered, over low heat for about 5 minutes.

3 Preheat the oven to 400 degrees. Wash and trim the zucchini, and cut them crosswise into slices about ¼ inch thick. Season with salt and pepper, and coat with all-purpose flour. In a skillet, heat 3 tbsp. of the oil over medium heat

and fry the zucchini until golden-brown. Remove from the pan and drain on kitchen paper.

4 Grease an ovenproof dish with the remaining oil. Arrange the zucchini on the bottom, pour over the tomato sauce and sprinkle with the grated cheese. Bake in the center of the oven for about 15 minutes, until golden-brown. Serve accompanied by potatoes.

Wine: Choose a robust red wine from Penedés to accompany this dish.

Note: This is delicious on its own or as an accompaniment to meat dishes; if serving as a side dish with a entrée, the quantities given above are enough for eight people.

Manchego

Don Quixote's native land, La Mancha, is also the home of queso manchego. Spain's most famous cheese. Manchego ewes have been bred in the region for centuries, and their milk, rich in fat, retains the flavor of the grass and wild herbs of the bleak pastures of La Mancha on which they graze.

Manchego cheese, with its distinctive black or yellow rind stamped with braiding, ranges in texture from mild and creamy to hard and crumbly. It is shaped into cylinders and left to ripen for two through 12 months, but can be purchased at various stages of maturity, from the fresh, pale yellow tierno and the delicately flavored semi-seco to the dry, dark-colored, mature seco whose taste is reminiscent of the best Parmesan. Anjejos, as the year-old cheese is known, has the strongest flavor. One variety is cured in olive oil for several months.

Manchego is a favorite with gourmets and much used in Spanish cuisine. It is eaten in tapas, served with chorizo or country ham, shredded over savory dishes, and even appreciated as a dessert with quince jelly.

Manchego, and a variety of other Spanish cheeses, is available at gourmet stores and by mail order.

Tortilla de patatas

Not difficult • Many regions

Potato omelet

Serves 4 to 6

3 cups potatoes
2 large onions
7 tbsp. olive oil
salt
freshly ground black pepper
6 eggs

Preparation time: 1 hour

*360 cal. per serving
(if serving 6)*

1 Peel and wash the potatoes, and cut them into thin slices. Peel the onions and dice.

2 Heat half the olive oil in a deep, heavy skillet about 8 inches in diameter. Add the potato slices and the chopped onion and cook over medium heat for about 25 minutes, until the potatoes are tender but not brown. Season with salt and pepper. When done, remove from the pan with a slotted spoon and allow to cool slightly.

3 Meanwhile, whisk the eggs in a bowl until foaming and season well with salt and pepper. Carefully stir in the potatoes and onions.

4 Heat the rest of the olive oil in the skillet over low heat. Add the egg-and-potato mixture (*above*), and cook for about 6 minutes, gently shaking the pan from time to time until the omelet begins to set.

5 Remove the pan from the heat, and place a flat plate on top of it (*above*).

Holding the plate in place with your hand, invert the pan and the plate, and tip the omelet out onto the plate, cooked side uppermost.

6 Carefully slide the omelet back into the pan (*above*), and cook it on the other side, adding a little more oil if necessary, for a further 6 to 8 minutes, or until cooked through.

7 Cut the omelet into wedges or cubes. Serve warm or cold.

Variation: Diced ham or sliced chorizo can be added to the beaten egg at the same time as the potatoes and onions.

Note: This simple but satisfying classic dish can be served as tapas, as an entrée or in between courses. Served with salad, it makes an ideal light supper for two. It has many variations, and the fillings can be a variety of vegetables, ham, or shrimp.

Piperrada

Not difficult • Basque Country

Mixed pepper omelet

Serves 4

2 medium-sized bell peppers,
1 red, 1 green
2 medium-sized beefsteak tomatoes
(about 1 ½ cups)
2 oz. ham
1 large onion
4 garlic cloves
3 tbsp. olive oil
salt
freshly ground black pepper
8 eggs

Preparation time: 45 minutes

450 cal. per serving

1 Heat the broiler or preheat the oven to 475 degrees. Wash the sweet peppers, wipe dry, and remove the skins (page 34, top recipe, Step 1). Halve the peppers, remove the ribs and seeds, and cut into narrow strips.

2 Meanwhile, plunge the tomatoes briefly into boiling water, skin, halve, and deseed them, and finely dice the flesh. Cut the ham into narrow strips. Peel and mince the onion and garlic.

3 Heat half the oil in a skillet over medium heat and sauté the onion, garlic, and ham until the onion is soft.

Add the tomatoes and bell peppers, season with salt and pepper, and sauté for a further 10 minutes until most of the liquid has evaporated. Transfer the mixture to a bowl.

4 Heat the rest of the olive oil in the skillet. Whisk the eggs, season with salt and pepper, and pour into the pan. Cook over low heat for about 3 minutes, stirring from time to time, until the eggs begin to set. Spread the vegetable-and-ham mixture over the egg, cover the pan, and cook for a further 10 minutes, until set. Serve hot with crusty white bread.

Huevos a la flamenca
Flamenco Eggs

Fairly easy • Andalucía

Serves 4

8 oz. potatoes
3 tbsp. olive oil
1 medium-sized onion
2 garlic cloves
2 bell pepper, 1 red, 1 green
5¼ oz. serrano ham (or prosciutto if unavailable)
1 chorizo, about 5½ oz. (see page 56)
1¼ lb. beefsteak tomatoes
1 cup freshly shelled peas
salt
freshly ground black pepper
1 tsp. mild paprika
8 eggs
Preparation time: about 1 hour
690 cal. per serving

1 Peel and wash the potatoes, then cut into small dice. Heat the olive oil in a large skillet over medium heat and fry the potatoes for about 5 minutes.

2 Peel and finely chop the onion and the garlic. Wash the bell peppers and remove the stalks, seeds and ribs, then chop into small dice. Add all the vegetables to the pan.

3 Preheat the oven to 350 degrees. Chop the ham into small pieces, slice the chorizo, and add them both to the skillet. Sauté for about 8 minutes.

4 Plunge the tomatoes into boiling water, then skin, halve, and deseed them. Coarsely chop the flesh. Add the peas and tomatoes to the pan. Season

with salt, pepper, and paprika. Stir, and cook for a further 5 minutes.

5 Grease a large baking dish and fill it with the vegetable mixture. Break each egg carefully into the dish and bake in the center of the oven for about 10 minutes, or until the eggs are set. If you like, sprinkle with a little more paprika, and serve with white bread.

Wine: A red or rosé wine from Navarre goes well with this dish.

Note: The combination of vegetables can be varied according to what is in season. If you prefer, you can divide the mixture into 4 dishes and break 2 eggs into each.

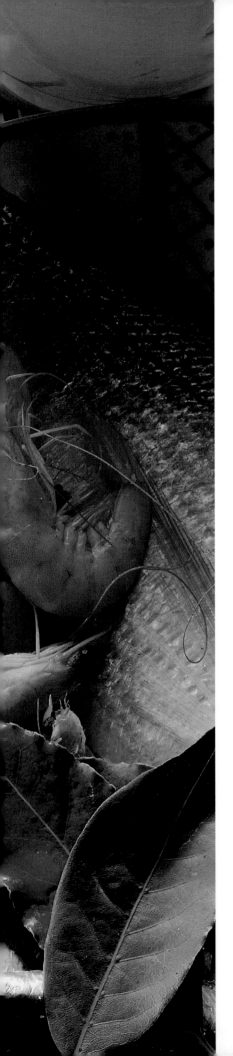

FISH AND SHELLFISH

With a coastline more than 1300 miles long, Spain enjoys a huge variety of fish or shellfish. To the north and west lie the stormy Bay of Biscay and the Atlantic; to the south there are the warmer waters of the Mediterranean. Streams and rivers yield delectable freshwater trout.

Regular deliveries from the coast to the bars and restaurants of Madrid testify to the Spanish love of seafood. After the Japanese, they are the world's greatest consumers of fish and shellfish, and in those areas where fresh seafood is less available, dried salt cod from the North Sea is a popular substitute. But this culinary passion for fish reaches its height around the coast, where the freshest possible seafood is available. In inland Spain, fish traditionally appears on a formal menu before the entrée, a meat course; on the coast, it often forms a meal in itself, in tapas, soups and entrées.

As a general rule, simple is best. Fish is often served broiled with a little oil or lightly fried. Shellfish, usually thought of as an appetizer, is likewise often broiled instead of steamed. As in all Spanish cooking, however, there are many regional specialties which are the subject of fierce pride and debate. The best scallops are alleged to come from Galicia; an authentic paella is only made in Valencia; while Catalonia lays claim to the *zarzuela*, an "operetta" of mixed seafood.

Zarzuela de mariscos

Shellfish Stew

Takes a little time • Catalonia

Serves 6

2 ¼ lb. beefsteak tomatoes
2 large onions
6 garlic cloves
1 fresh, or dried, chili pepper (see Glossary)
3 ½ oz. lean bacon
7 tbsp. olive oil
½ cup ground almonds
pinch of powdered saffron
4 bay leaves
1 sprig thyme
1 sprig rosemary
2 cups dry white wine
juice of ½ lemon
salt
freshly ground black pepper
1 ¼ lb. large clams
1 ¼ lb. small clams
6 large, fresh, unpeeled jumbo shrimp
12 cleaned scallops, without shells
14 oz. cleaned squid
3 lemons

Preparation time: 1 ½ hours

570 cal. per serving

1 Plunge the tomatoes briefly into boiling water. Skin, halve, and deseed them, and coarsely chop the flesh. Peel and mince the onions and garlic. Wash the chili pepper. If fresh, deseed and cut into thin rings; if dried, crush with the back of a spoon. Cut the bacon into small dice.

2 In a large saucepan, heat the oil. Sauté the onions, garlic, and chili pepper over medium heat, until the onions are transparent. Stir in the bacon. Add the tomatoes, reduce the heat to low, and simmer gently for about 10 minutes.

3 Add the ground almonds, saffron powder, bay leaves, thyme, and rosemary to the pan. Pour in the white wine and 2 cups water. Stir in the lemon juice, and season with salt and pepper. Bring to a boil, then reduce the heat to low, cover, and simmer for about 15 minutes more.

4 Meanwhile, thoroughly scrub the two types of clam with a brush under cold running water (*above*). Discard any that are already open.

5 Add the clams to the other ingredients in the saucepan. Replace the lid and cook until the shells open, about 5 minutes. Discard any that remain closed.

6 Wash and dry the shrimp and scallops. Cut the squid into thin rings (*above*) and add together with the shrimp and scallops to the pan. Continue to cook, covered, over low heat for a further 10 minutes.

7 Cut the lemons lengthwise into wedges. Check the zarzuela for seasoning and adjust if necessary. Serve straight from the pan in which it was cooked, with the lemon wedges and crusty white bread.

Wine: A dry, white Penedés from Catalonia goes particularly well with zarzuela.

Note: Because guests use their fingers to eat this dish, provide everyone with a small finger-bowl of warm water containing a slice of lemon, the table napkins should be large! Zarzuela is also the name for a satirical Spanish operetta.

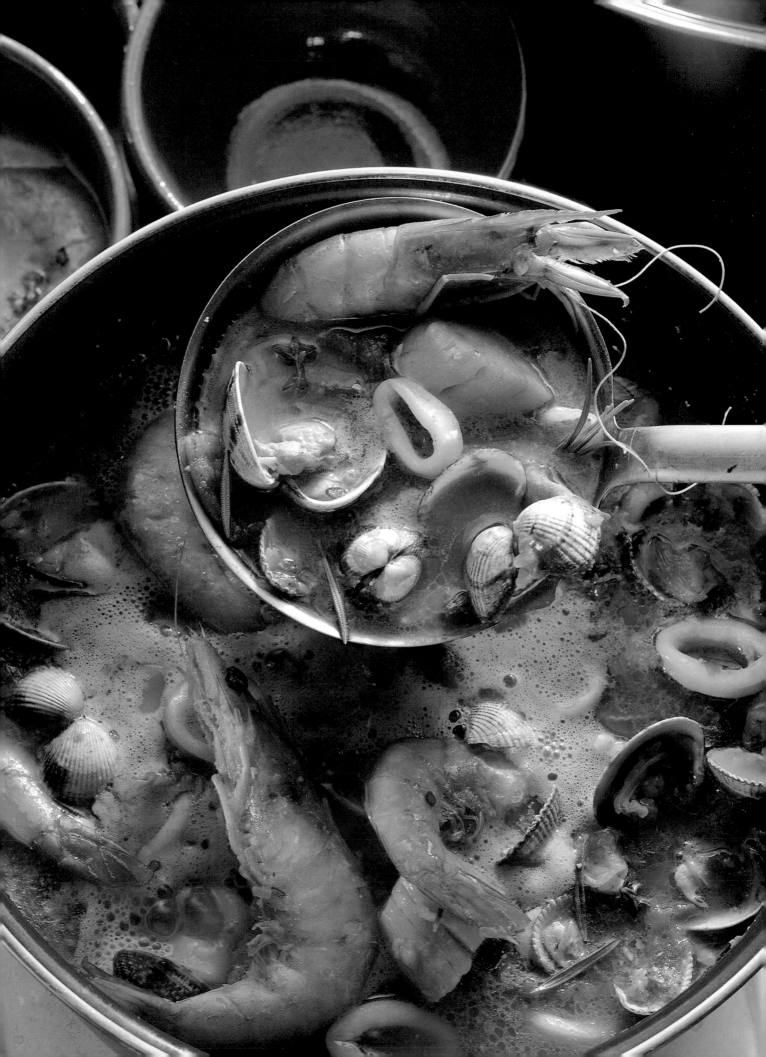

Vieiras a la gallega

Baked Scallops

Not difficult • Galicia

Serves 4

16 cleaned scallops, including coral
juice of 1 lemon
1 onion
4 tbsp. olive oil
2 garlic cloves
3 tbsp. aguardiente de orujo
or grappa (see Note)
1 tsp. mild paprika
cayenne pepper
ground cinnamon
salt
freshly ground black pepper
⅔ cup dry white wine
1 small bunch flat-leaved parsley
(about 1 oz.)
4 tbsp. fresh bread crumbs

Preparation time: 45 minutes

260 cal. per serving

1 Rinse the scallops under running water and pat dry. Separate the white flesh and the pink coral. Finely chop the coral, sprinkle the white flesh with lemon juice and set both aside. Preheat the oven to 400 degrees.

2 Peel and finely chop the onion. In a large saucepan, heat 1 tbsp. of the olive oil and sauté the onion over medium heat until transparent. Peel and crush the garlic into the onion. Stir in the scallop coral. Pour in the aguardiente and season with the paprika, a little cayenne pepper, cinnamon, salt, and pepper. Add the white wine, bring to a boil, then remove from the heat.

3 Wash the parsley, shake dry, and remove the stalks. Finely chop the leaves and mix with the bread crumbs. Arrange the scallops in oiled individual shells or in a single layer in an oiled baking dish.

4 Pour the sauce over the scallops and top evenly with the bread crumb and parsley mixture. Sprinkle with the rest of the oil and bake in the center of the oven for 10 to 12 minutes, until golden-brown. Serve with crusty white bread.

Wine: A dry white wine from Galicia, goes extremely well with this dish.

Note: Try and buy fresh scallops opened and cleaned, and attached to the flat half-shell, Ask for the rounded top shells, which make attractive individual "dishes." Clean them by scrubbing vigorously with a nailbrush under cold running water. Aguardiente de orujo is a strong Spanish spirit distilled from grape skins, similar to grappa and marc.

Lemons

It is hard to imagine Spanish cooking without the lemon. The tart juice enhances the flavor of fish, grilled meat, stews, vegetable dishes and salads. In appetizers, it helps sharpen the appetite; in desserts or drinks, its clean taste refreshes the palate after a meal. Sliced or cut into wedges, it makes a bright, attractive garnish for a wide range of dishes.

The lemon tree, like most citrus fruits, originated in southeast Asia. It was introduced to North Africa and Spain by the Moors between A.D. 1000 and 1200, and later spread all round the Mediterranean, whose climate was well suited to its cultivation. In Spain, about 375,000 acres are devoted to lemon orchards and the trees do particularly well in the southern coastal regions of the Levant – Valencia and Murcia – and Andalucía. Spain is a major exporter of lemons to northern Europe.

Lemon trees grow to a height of between 4 and 7 feet and are characterized by sharp thorns, dark evergreen leaves, and fragrant white blossom. The trees bloom and fruit throughout the year. The juicy yellow fruit is a valuable source of vitamin C, which aids metabolism and strengthens the body's natural defenses against disease.

Salmón a la Ribereña

Simple • Asturias

Salmon with Ham and Cider Sauce

Serves 4

4 salmon steaks (about 7 oz. each)
juice of ½ lemon
salt
2 oz. serrano ham
(or prosciutto if unavailable)
6 tbsp. all-purpose flour
4 tbsp. olive oil
freshly ground white pepper
1 cup Asturian
or other strong dry cider

Preparation time: 45 minutes

290 cal. per serving

1 Rinse the salmon steaks under cold running water and pat dry. Place in a dish, sprinkle both sides with the lemon juice, and season lightly with salt. Leave to marinate for about 15 minutes. Meanwhile, finely dice the ham.

2 Put the flour on a plate and dip the salmon steaks in it to coat them, shaking off any excess. Heat the olive oil in a skillet and fry the salmon over medium heat for about 4 minutes on each side. Season lightly with white pepper, then remove from the pan and keep warm.

3 Sauté the diced ham in the oil remaining in the pan for about 5 minutes. Add the cider and cook over high heat until reduced by about one third. Season with pepper.

4 Arrange the salmon on warmed plates and pour the sauce over it. Serve with cooked spinach.

Note: Asturian cider is the best drink to go with this dish; otherwise, any dry cider, or a white wine, is suitable.

Besugo al horno

Takes a little time • Andalucía

Baked Sea Bream

Serves 4

1 untreated lemon
1 cleaned sea bream (about 2½ lb.)
salt
freshly ground white pepper
1 lb. 5 oz. potatoes (evenly small)
1 onion
4 garlic cloves
1 large beefsteak tomato
2 tsp. fresh thyme leaves
⅓ cup olive oil
1 cup dry white wine
olive oil
1 small bunch flat-leaved parsley
(about 1 oz.)
2 tbsp. fresh bread crumbs

Preparation time: 1 ½ hours

790 cal. per serving

1 Scrub the lemon under hot running water. Cut in half lengthwise, cut one half into 4 wedges and set aside. Squeeze the juice from the other half.

2 Rinse the fish, pat dry, sprinkle inside and out with the lemon juice, and season with salt and pepper. Make 4 diagonal incisions in the fish with a sharp knife and insert the lemon wedges. Preheat the oven to 350 degrees.

3 Peel and thinly slice the potatoes. Peel and halve the onion, and cut into thin rings. Put potatoes and onions in a bowl. Peel the garlic, crush 2 cloves into the bowl, and reserve the others.

4 Plunge the tomato briefly into boiling water. Skin, halve, and deseed it. Coarsely chop the flesh, and add to the potatoes. Add the thyme, season with salt and pepper, and stir thoroughly.

5 Grease a baking dish with a little of the olive oil and arrange the vegetables on the bottom. Pour over the white wine and the remaining oil. Lay the fish on top.

6 Wash the parsley, shake dry, and remove the stalks. Chop the leaves finely and place in a bowl with the bread crumbs. Crush in the remaining garlic, season with salt and pepper, mix, and spread over the fish.

7 Place the dish in the center of the oven and bake for about 50 minutes. The fish is cooked if it feels firm when pressed with a finger.

Merluza con alcaparras

Fairly easy • Catalonia **Hake with Caper Sauce**   *Serves 4*

1 garlic head
4 hake filets (each about 7 oz. each)
salt
freshly ground black pepper
1 tbsp. olive oil
¾ cup dry white wine
1 small onion
½ cup almonds
4 tbsp. capers

Preparation time: 45 minutes

380 cal. per serving

1 Preheat the oven to 350 degrees. Place the garlic on a rack or griddle in the center of the oven and roast for 15 to 20 minutes.

2 Rinse the fish under cold running water, pat dry, and season with salt and pepper. Grease an ovenproof baking dish with the oil, arrange the fish steaks side by side in the bottom, and pour the white wine over them. Cover and bake in the center of the oven for about 20 minutes.

3 Meanwhile, peel and coarsely chop the onion. Blanch the almonds (see page 50, Step 1) and toast them in a dry skillet over low heat until golden.

Carefully peel the garlic cloves and crush them and the almonds, onion, and 3 tbsp. of the capers in a mortar with a pestle or in a food processor.

4 Remove the fish from the baking dish with a fish slice or slotted spoon and keep warm. Bring the broth left in the dish to a boil, then reduce the heat to low. Stir in the almond paste, season with salt and pepper, and continue to cook until hot. Transfer the fish to four serving plates and pour the sauce over it. Garnish with the rest of the capers and serve with vegetables.

Wine: A dry white wine from Valencia is excellent with this dish.

Marmitako

Fairly easy • Basque Country

Tuna Casserole

1 large onion
4 garlic cloves
1 large red bell pepper
1 large green bell pepper
1 ¼ lb. beefsteak tomatoes
2 tbsp. olive oil
1 fresh chili pepper (see Glossary)
salt
freshly ground black pepper
2 tsp. mild paprika
14 oz. potatoes
1 cup dry white wine
1 lb. 5 oz. fresh tuna
juice of 1 lemon

Preparation time: 1 ½ hours

570 cal. per serving

1 Peel and finely chop the onion. Peel the garlic. Wash the red and green peppers, halve, remove the ribs and seeds, and cut the flesh into narrow strips. Plunge the tomatoes briefly into boiling water. Skin, halve, deseed, and coarsely chop the flesh.

2 Heat the olive oil in a large flameproof casserole or heavy saucepan. Sauté the onion until soft. Crush the garlic into the pan, stir in the peppers, and sauté for about 5 minutes more.

3 Wash the chili pepper and deseed it. Cut it into thin strips and add to the casserole. Season with salt and pepper, and the paprika. Stir thoroughly, cover the pan, and cook over low heat for about 10 minutes.

4 Peel the potatoes and cut into ⅜ inch dice. Stir the white wine and diced potatoes into the casserole. Cover and simmer over low heat for about 25 minutes.

5 Rinse the tuna under cold running water and pat dry. Cut it into cubes the same size as the potatoes. Sprinkle the fish with the lemon juice, season with salt and pepper, and add to the casserole. Cover and cook for a further 5 minutes. Check the seasoning and adjust if necessary. Serve with crusty white bread.

Wine: Serve with a dry white wine from the Basque Country.

Dorada al sal

Gilt-head Bream in a Salt Crust

Not difficult • Andalucía

Serves 4

*1 gilt-head bream,
cleaned (about 2 lb. 10 oz.)
juice of ½ lemon
salt
freshly ground white pepper
1 sprig thyme
3 garlic cloves
4 ½ lb. coarse (kosher) sea salt
2 untreated lemons
For the Romesco Sauce:
2 tbsp. almonds
1 large beef tomato
3 garlic cloves
salt
freshly ground black pepper
cayenne pepper
1 tbsp. red wine vinegar*

Preparation time: 1 hour

570 cal. per serving

1 Preheat the oven to 475 degrees. Rinse the fish thoroughly under cold running water and pat dry. Sprinkle with the lemon juice inside and out, and season with salt and white pepper. Rinse the thyme and pat dry. Peel the garlic and halve each clove lengthwise. Place the thyme and garlic inside the fish (*above*).

2 Pour half the sea salt into a roasting pan or ovenproof dish and spread in an even layer over the bottom. Lay the fish on top.

3 Sprinkle the rest of the salt over the fish, so that it is completely covered (*above*). Place in the center of the oven and bake for 35 to 40 minutes.

4 Meanwhile, prepare the Romesco Sauce. Blanch the almonds (Page 50,

Step 1) and toast them briefly in a dry skillet until golden (*above*). Plunge the tomato briefly into boiling water; skin, halve, and deseed. Peel the garlic. Grind the almonds, tomatoes, and garlic together in a food processor or vegetable mill.

5 Season with plenty of salt and black pepper, and add some cayenne pepper and the wine vinegar. Stir in the oil.

6 Remove the fish from the oven and break off the salt crust (*above*). Lift the fish carefully out of the dish, skin it, and gently pull the flesh away from the bones into fillets. Serve with the Romesco Sauce and the lemons cut into wedges. Accompany with a side dish of potatoes.

Wine: Choose a dry white wine, such as an Albariño from Galicia.

Truchas a la navarra

Quick and easy • Navarre

Trout Stuffed with Ham

Serves 4

4 cleaned trout (about 12 oz. each)
salt
freshly ground black pepper
4 slices (about 5 ½ oz. total) serrano ham
(or prosciutto if unavailable)
all-purpose flour
3 ½ oz. fatty bacon
5 tbsp. olive oil
1 untreated lemon

Preparation time: 25 minutes

710 cal. per serving

1 Rinse the trout under cold running water, pat dry, and season lightly inside and out with salt and pepper. Place a folded slice of ham inside each fish.

2 Spread some all-purpose flour on a plate and turn each trout in the all-purpose flour to coat it evenly, shaking to remove any excess.

3 Finely dice the bacon. Heat the oil in a skillet and fry the bacon over low heat until it has rendered up most of its fat.

4 Add the trout to the pan and fry them for about 10 minutes, turning once, until golden-brown all over. Transfer to a warmed serving platter, sprinkle the bacon on top and garnish with the lemon cut into wedges. Serve with potatoes or crusty white bread.

Wine: This dish goes very well with a Navarre rosé.

Variation: If you prefer, serve the trout without sprinkling with the bacon. In Asturias, the serrano ham is omitted.

Bacalao al pil-pil

Fairly easy • Basque Country

Salt Cod in Olive Oil and Garlic Sauce

Serves 4

1 lb. 5 oz. dried salt cod (see Glossary)
1 garlic head
1 ¼ cups olive oil
1 dried chili pepper (see Glossary)
freshly ground white pepper

Preparation time: 35 minutes (plus 24 hours soaking time)

1,200 cal. per serving

1 Soak the salt cod in cold water for at least 24 hours, changing the water three or four times. The fish should roughly double in size.

2 Remove the cod from the water and rinse thoroughly. Bone if necessary, taking care not to damage the skin, and cut into serving portions. Peel and thinly slice the garlic.

3 Heat the oil in a sauté pan or flameproof casserole with a handle. Crush the chili pepper with the back of a spoon and add to the pan with the garlic. Fry over low heat until the garlic is golden, then remove both garlic and chili pepper with a slotted spoon. Reserve the garlic and discard the chili pepper.

4 Lay the salt cod, skin downward, in the olive oil and cook slowly over low heat for about 20 minutes. Constantly shake the pan, so that the fish juices and the oil combine and thicken into a mayonnaise-like sauce. Lightly season the fish and sauce with white pepper.

5 Transfer the fish and sauce to four warmed plates or pottery bowls, garnish with the reserved garlic slices, and serve immediately, accompanied by potatoes or crusty white bread.

Wine: Choose a dry white wine from the Basque Country.

Note: Bacalao al pil-pil is also good served cold.

Almejas a la marinera

Simple • Galicia **Clams Fisherman-style** *Serves 4 to 6*

1 small onion
2 garlic cloves
1 lb. 5 oz. beefsteak tomatoes
2 tbsp. olive oil
1 cup dry white wine
1 bay leaf
salt
freshly ground black pepper
2 ¼ lb. clams
small bunch flat-leaved parsley
(about 1 oz.)

Preparation time: 1 hour

170 cal. per serving
(if serving 6)

1 Peel and mince the onion and garlic. Plunge the tomatoes briefly into boiling water; skin and halve them, deseed, and finely chop the flesh.

2 Heat the olive oil in a large saucepan and sauté the onion and garlic over low heat until the onion is soft. Add the chopped tomatoes, white wine, and bay leaf. Season with salt and pepper. Simmer, uncovered, over low heat for about 10 minutes.

3 Meanwhile, thoroughly scrub the clams under cold running water, discarding any that are already open.

4 Add the clams to the pan, cover, and cook over high heat for 5 to 8 minutes, shaking the pan from time to time. Discard the bay leaf and any clams that remain closed after cooking.

5 Wash the parsley, shake dry, remove the stalks, and chop the leaves finely. Transfer the clams and sauce to a serving dish, sprinkle with the chopped parsley, and serve with crusty bread.

Note: Any type of clam, as well as oysters and mussels can be prepared in the same way.

Tumbet de pescado mallorquín

Fish Hotpot

Takes time • Majorca

Serves 4

8 tbsp. olive oil
1 lb. 10 oz. cod fillet
salt
freshly ground black pepper
juice of 1 lemon
½ cup dry white wine
2 red bell peppers
(about 10 ½ oz.)
1¼ lb. potatoes
2 eggplant (about 14 oz.)
all-purpose flour
1 large onion
2 garlic cloves
1 lb. 10 oz. beefsteak tomatoes
2 bay leaves
pinch of ground cinnamon
1 tsp. sugar

Preparation time: 1 ½ hours

520 cal. per serving

1 Preheat the oven to 350 degrees. Brush an ovenproof dish with a little oil and lay the fish in it. Season with salt and pepper, and sprinkle with the lemon juice and wine. Bake in the oven for about 10 minutes. Remove the fish and reserve the pan juices.

2 Increase the oven temperature to 425 degrees and skin the bell peppers, following the instructions in Step 1, top recipe, on page 34. Meanwhile, peel the potatoes and cut them into thin slices. Heat 3 tbsp. of the oil in a pan and fry the potatoes for about 5 minutes. Add 1 cup water, cover, and cook over low heat for a further 15 minutes. Drain and reserve.

3 Wash, trim, and thickly slice the eggplant. Coat in all-purpose flour and fry in 3 tbsp. of the oil over medium heat until golden-brown on both sides. Season with salt and pepper, and reserve.

4 Peel and finely chop the onion and garlic. Heat 2 tbsp. of the olive oil in a heavy pan and sauté the onion and garlic until the onion is soft. Plunge the tomatoes briefly into boiling water, skin and halve them, deseed, and coarsely chop the flesh.

5 Add the tomatoes to the pan and stir in the fish pan juices, the bay leaves, the cinnamon and the sugar. Season with salt and pepper, cover, and simmer over medium heat for about 15 minutes. Discard the bay leaves and purée the rest in a food processor.

6 Oil an ovenproof dish. Arrange half the potatoes on the bottom, then half the fish, eggplant and peppers. Repeat, adding a second layer of potatoes, fish, eggplant, and peppers. Pour the puréed sauce over the dish and bake for about 15 minutes. Serve hot.

Wine: This dish goes well with a white Muscatel from Majorca.

MEAT AND GAME

Roasted, broiled, barbecued, fried or served as spicy sausages or hearty stews, meat is the mainstay of Spanish cookery. As in other mountainous regions, much of this meat comes from smaller animals such as pigs, goats, and sheep; these animals are less expensive to raise than cattle, which requite extensive grazing. There is also a good supply of game in the wild.

Lamb was the staple of the Moorish diet, as the Moors did not eat pork; pork came into its own in Christian Spain. Today, no part of the pig is wasted. Apart from prime cuts, many kinds of sausages and hams are made and even the feet, tails, and ears are eaten. This waste-not, want-not attitude is also reflected in the extensive consumption of organ meats such as tripe. Meat is frequently grilled, broiled, barbecued, or roasted, cooking methods that depend for success on tender succulent meat from young animals. Those that provide the renowned lamb and pork roasts of central Spain, for example, are sometimes little more than a few weeks old. Veal is more commonly used than beef, and cows are grazed more for their milk than meat. There are interesting regional variations in meat dishes. In Catalonia, beef may be cooked with chocolate; in Asturias, pork is baked in cider. However they are prepared, meat dishes are usually served with simple side dishes such as fried potatoes or fresh bread.

Ternera "La Mancha"

Veal and Vegetable Casserole

Not difficult • La Mancha

Serves 4

4 veal scallops (about 6 ½ oz. each)
juice of ½ lemon
salt
freshly ground black pepper
1 large onion
2 green bell peppers (about 10 ½ oz.)
2 medium-sized beefsteak tomatoes (about 14 oz.)
3 garlic cloves
4 tbsp. olive oil
3/4 cup meat broth

Preparation time: 1 hour

330 cal. per serving

1 Pound the scallops with a steak hammer to flatten them. Sprinkle both sides with the lemon juice, and season with salt and pepper. Cover and leave to stand.

2 Peel and finely chop the onion. Wash the green peppers, halve them, remove the stalks, ribs and seeds, and dice the flesh. Plunge tomatoes briefly into boiling water. Skin, halve, and deseed them and finely dice the flesh. Mix together in a bowl with the onion and peppers.

3 Peel and crush the garlic and stir it into the vegetables. Season with plenty of salt and pepper.

4 Arrange half the vegetables in the bottom of a large flameproof casserole. Moisten with a little of the olive oil and some broth. Cover, and cook over low heat for about 40 minutes, until the meat is tender. Serve with crusty white bread.

Wine: A light red wine from La Mancha goes particularly well with this dish.

Note: The dish can also be baked in the oven at about 350 degrees.

Chuletas al estilo de Aragón

Pork Chop and Potato Bake

Not difficult • Aragón

Serves 4

1 lb. 12 oz. potatoes
2 tbsp. olive oil
salt
freshly ground black pepper
1 ¼ cups dry white wine
4 pork chops (about 6 ½ oz. each)
4 tbsp. coarsely chopped almonds
4 garlic cloves
1 small bunch flat-leaved parsley (about 1 oz.)
2 eggs

Preparation time: 1 ½ hours

760 cal. per serving

1 Peel and wash the potatoes, and cut into slices ¼ inch thick. Brush an ovenproof casserole or roasting pan with half the olive oil. Spread the sliced potatoes in a layer over the bottom of the pan, season with salt and pepper, and pour the wine over them.

2 Preheat the oven to 400 degrees. Season both sides of the chops with salt and pepper, then lay them on top of the potatoes.

3 Heat the remaining oil in a skillet and fry the almonds until golden; transfer to a bowl. Peel the garlic and crush it over the almonds. Wash and dry the parsley and remove the stalks; finely chop the leaves. Mix with the almonds and garlic, season with salt and pepper, and spread over the chops.

4 Cover the casserole and bake in the center of the oven for about 45 minutes, or until the potatoes have absorbed all the liquid.

5 Meanwhile, hard boil the eggs for about 10 minutes. Plunge them into cold water, shell them and chop finely. Serve the chops and potatoes hot, sprinkled with the chopped egg.

Wine: Choose a dry white wine.

Estofado a la andaluza

Ragout of Beef

Takes time • Andalusia

Serves 4

1 garlic head
1 lb. 12 oz. boned shoulder of beef
1 large green bell pepper
2 beefsteak tomatoes
(about 10 ½ oz.)
2 large onions
2 medium-sized carrots
(about 7 oz.)
2 tsp. peppercorns
large pinch of saffron
½ tsp. ground cinnamon
salt
3 tbsp. olive oil • 2 bay leaves
½ cup dry white wine
4 potatoes (about 1 ¼ lb.)
1 small bunch flat-leaved parsley
(about 1 oz.)
freshly ground black pepper

Preparation time: 2 hours

550 cal. per serving

1 Preheat the oven to 400 degrees. Reserve 2 cloves of the garlic, and roast the rest in the center of the oven for about 20 minutes.

2 Meanwhile, cut the meat into 1-inch dice. Wash and halve the green pepper, remove the stalk, ribs and seeds, and cut into narrow strips. Plunge the tomatoes into boiling water, skin and cut into eighths. Peel the onions and cut into thin rings and chop the rings in half. Peel and slice the carrots. Put the meat and vegetables into a flameproof casserole or heavy pan and stir to mix.

3 Peel the raw garlic cloves and grind them and the peppercorns in a mortar with a pestle or in a food processor. Add the saffron and cinnamon. Squeeze the roasted garlic cloves from their skins

and add to the spices. Season with salt and mix into a paste.

4 Mix the paste with 7 tablespoons water and the oil, and add to the casserole with the bay leaves. Add the wine, bring to a boil, reduce the heat to low, cover and simmer for about 1 ½ hours.

5 Peel the potatoes and cut into 1-inch dice. Stir them into the stew about 20 minutes before the end of the cooking time. Wash the parsley, pat dry, remove the stalks, and mince the leaves. When the meat is tender, discard the bay leaves. Season with salt and freshly ground pepper and stir in the parsley. Serve with crusty white bread.

Wine: The dish goes well with a strong red wine, such as a Navarre or a Rioja.

Solomillo a la malagueña

Not difficult • Andalusia

Roast Loin of Pork Malaga-style

Serves 4

2 tbsp. olive oil
1 lb. 12 oz. loin of pork
salt
freshly ground black pepper
¾ cup Málaga or other dessert wine
½ cup meat broth
1 x 2-inch piece cinnamon stick
2 tbsp. Málaga or other raisins
½ cup almonds

Preparation time: 1 ½ hours

670 cal. per serving

1 Preheat the oven to 350 degrees.

2 On top of the stove, heat the olive oil in a large flameproof casserole over high heat, until a haze forms above the surface. Add the meat and sear until brown all over. Remove from the heat. Season with salt and black pepper. Add the wine and broth to the pot, then the cinnamon stick and raisins. Cover the casserole and cook in the center of the oven for about 1 hour, until tender.

3 Meanwhile, blanch the almonds (see page 50, Step 1) and toast them in a dry skillet over medium heat until golden. Reserve half and grind the rest

with a pestle in a mortar or in a food processor.

4 Remove the meat from the casserole and keep warm. Discard the cinnamon and stir the ground almonds into the pan juices. Bring to a boil on top of the stove. Reduce the heat to low and simmer, uncovered, for about 5 minutes, adjusting the seasoning if necessary. Meanwhile, slice the meat and arrange it on a serving dish. Pour the sauce over it and sprinkle with the reserved almonds. Serve immediately, accompanied by rice and vegetables.

Wine: A dry rosé from Catalonia goes well with this dish.

Ternera a la sevillana

Not difficult · Andalusia

Roast Veal Seville-style

Serves 4

2 beefsteak tomatoes (about 10 ½
oz.)
2 large onions
1 garlic clove
1 lb. 12 oz. boned shoulder of veal
salt
freshly ground black pepper
2 tbsp. olive oil
½ cup meat broth
1 x 2-inch piece cinnamon stick
3 tbsp. slivered almonds
4 tbsp. pitted green olives

Preparation time: 1 ½ hours
400 cal. per serving

1 Plunge the tomatoes briefly into boiling water. Skin and halve them, deseed, and coarsely chop the flesh. Peel and finely chop the onions. Peel the garlic clove and cut in half lengthwise. Preheat the oven to 450 degrees.

2 Wash the meat, pat dry, and rub all over with salt and pepper. heat the oil in a shallow flameproof casserole or roasting pan over high heat and sear the meat until brown all over. Reduce heat to medium, add the onion and garlic to the pan oil and cook until soft.

3 Pour over the white wine and cook until slightly reduced. Add the broth and chopped tomatoes. season with salt and pepper, and add the cinnamon stick.

4 In a dry skillet, toast the almond slivers until golden-brown.

5 Remove the meat from the roasting pan and keep warm. Discard the cinnamon stick and set the roasting pan over low heat. Stir the almonds and olives into the pan juices and simmer for about 5 minutes, adding more seasoning if necessary. Slice the meat onto warmed serving dish, pour over the sauce and serve, accompanied by saffron rice (see page 105, Note).

Rabo de toro a la sevillana

Takes time · Andalusia

Braised Oxtail Seville-style

Serves 4

1 large onion
1 small leek
1 large carrot
3 ½ oz. celery root
4 garlic cloves · 5 tbsp. olive oil
3 lb. 5 oz. oxtail, cut into pieces
2 tbsp. tomato paste
1 cup dry red wine
1 ¾ cup meat broth
2 bay leaves
1 sprig thyme · 3 cloves
salt
freshly ground black pepper
3 tbsp. dry fino sherry

Preparation time: 3 ½ hours

760 cal. per serving

1 Preheat the oven to 300 degrees.

2 Peel and coarsely chop the onion. Trim and wash the leek, and cut into thin rings. Peel the carrot and celery root, and cut into small pieces. Peel and crush the garlic cloves.

3 Heat the oil in a flameproof casserole over high heat until a haze forms above the surface, then quickly sear the oxtail until brown all over. Add the chopped vegetables and crushed garlic and sauté, stirring constantly, for about 5 minutes.

4 Stir in the tomato paste. Add the red wine and the broth. Add the bay leaves, thyme, and cloves. season with salt and pepper. Cover tightly and cook in the center of the oven for about 2 ½ hours, or until tender, adding a little water if too much liquid evaporates.

5 Remove the oxtail with a slotted spoon. Discard bones and keep the meat warm. Strain the pan juices through a fine sieve into a saucepan. Stir in the sherry. Place over medium heat and cook, uncovered, until the sauce reduces by about half. Check the seasoning and add more salt and pepper if necessary. Serve the oxtail in the sauce, accompanied by potatoes or crusty white bread.

Wine: A strong red Rioja goes particularly well with this dish.

Lenguas con salsa de granada

Takes time • Andalusia

Calf's Tongue with Pomegranate Sauce

Serves 4

2 small fresh calf's tongues (about 1¼ lb. each) or 4 pig's tongues (about 12 oz. each)
salt
2 pomegranates (or, if unavailable, 5 to 6 tbsp. grenadine syrup)
1 large onion
1 tbsp. olive oil
8 tbsp. dry (fino) sherry
¾ cup meat broth
freshly ground black pepper

Preparation time: about 2 hours (plus 2½ hours soaking and cooling time)

500 cal. per serving

1 Soak the tongues in cold water for about 2 hours, then drain. Transfer to a pan of fresh cold water, bring to a boil, to remove impurities and drain.

2 Bring a pan of slightly salted water to a boil, and add the tongues. Cool, then trim off any gristle or fat from the base, loosen the skin with the tip of a knife, and peel with your fingers (*above*).

3 Meanwhile, cut the pomegranates in

half crosswise and scoop out the seeds with a spoon (*above*). Peel and mince the onion.

4 Heat the olive oil in a saucepan and sauté the onion until soft. Add the sherry to the pan. Reserve 2 tbsp. of the pomegranate seeds and add the rest to the pan (or, if using, pour in the grenadine syrup.) Add the broth and simmer for about 20 minutes. Season with salt and black pepper.

5 Slice the tongues across the grain (see above). Strain the sauce through a sieve into a large saucepan and heat through. Check the seasoning and adjust if necessary. Add the tongues and simmer over low heat for about 15 minutes. Transfer to a warmed serving dish and sprinkle with the reserved pomegranate seeds. Serve with saffron rice (see Note).

Wine: Dry sherry or manzanilla goes well with this dish.

Variation: Tongue with walnut sauce
Omit the pomegranate sauce and instead simmer 1 chopped garlic clove, 2 skinned, deseeded and chopped tomatoes and 6 tbsp. chopped walnuts in ¾ cup dry white wine for 20 minutes. Season with salt and pepper, then add the tongue to the sauce as in Step 5.

Note: To make saffron rice, fry 1 small minced onion in 1½ tbsp. olive oil in a large sauté pan until soft. Add 1¼ cups round-grain rice and stir for 2 to 3 minutes without browning. Add 3 cups boiling water, 1 tbsp. salt and ¼ tsp. saffron. Bring back to a boil, stir, then simmer over very low heat until all liquid is absorbed, about 20 minutes. Fluff with a fork before serving.

Cordero a la castellana

Simple but takes time • Castile **Castilian lamb** *Serves 4*

4 lamb shanks (about 1 lb. each)
2 cups dry white wine
3 tbsp. white wine vinegar
3 bay leaves
1 sprig thyme
1 sprig rosemary
6 juniper berries
1 tbsp. black peppercorns
1 large onion
4 garlic cloves
2 carrots
1 large beefsteak tomato
salt

Preparation time: 1½ hours
(plus 12 hours marinating time)

1,200 cal. per serving

1 Place the lamb shanks or chops in a single layer in dish. Pour the wine and vinegar to just cover the meat. Add the bay leaves, thyme, rosemary, juniper berries, and peppercorns.

2 Peel and finely chop the onion and garlic. Peel the carrots and dice finely. Plunge the tomato briefly into boiling water, skin and halve it, deseed, and coarsely chop the flesh. Mix the vegetables together, season with salt, and spread them over the lamb.

3 Cover and refrigerate for at least 12 hours, or overnight.

4 When you are ready to cook, transfer the contents of the bowl to a flameproof casserole or heavy saucepan. Bring to a boil, reduce the heat to very low, cover and simmer for about 1 ½ hours, or until tender. Serve the lamb in the pan juices, accompanied by boiled potatoes.

Wine: A dry white wine goes well with this dish.

Variation: If you like, you can add some cooked white beans to the other vegetables. Serve with crusty white bread.

Conejo al estilo morisco

Not difficult • Andalusia   **Moorish Style Rabbit Casserole**   *Serves 6*

1 rabbit (about 4 lb. 8 oz.)
2 ¼ lb. onions
1 garlic head
5 tbsp. olive oil
salt
freshly ground black pepper
large pinch of saffron
1 cup dry white wine
2 tbsp. raisins

Preparation time: 1 ½ hours

790 cal. per serving

1 Cut the rabbit into 6 servings (or ask the butcher to do it for you). Preheat the oven to 325 degrees. Peel the onions and slice into rings. Peel and thinly slice the garlic cloves.

2 Heat the olive oil in a flameproof casserole over high heat until a haze forms above the surface. Fry the rabbit pieces until brown all over. Remove from the pan with a slotted spoon, season with plenty of salt and pepper, and set aside.

3 In the fat left in the casserole, sauté the onion over low heat until soft. Remove half and reserve. Spread the remainder over the bottom of the casserole and place the rabbit pieces on top. Mix the garlic with the rest of the onions and spread the mixture over the rabbit.

4 Cover and bake in the center of the oven for about 20 minutes. Mix the saffron with the white wine and pour over the rabbit. Sprinkle with the raisins. Cover and continue to cook for a further 25 minutes. Serve with crusty white bread.

Variation: Hunter-style rabbit
Cut the rabbit into serving portions and fry in hot oil until golden-brown. Add 1 minced onion and 2 minced garlic cloves. Add a little white wine, 3 coarsely chopped tomatoes, 2 tsp. thyme, 1 bay leaf, and a sprig of rosemary. Bring to a boil, cover, and cook for about 30 minutes. Halfway through the cooking time, stir in 2 cups halved button mushrooms. Check for seasoning, and serve sprinkled with chopped parsley.

Solomillo de cerdo con jamón

Fairly easy • Extremadura   **Pork Loin with Ham**   *Serves 6*

2 ¼ lb. loin of pork
salt
freshly ground black pepper
1 tsp. mild paprika
8 oz. medium-thick slices serrano ham (or prosciutto if unavailable)
1 ¼ lb. pearl onions or shallots
2 tbsp. olive oil
7 tbsp. dry (fino) sherry
1 cup meat broth

Preparation time: 1 ½ hours

450 cal. per serving

1 Rinse the pork under cold running water and pat dry. Mix some salt and pepper with the paprika and rub all over the outside of the meat. Preheat the oven to 350 degrees.

2 Lay half the ham slices side-by-side to form a long rectangle. Place the pork on top and lay the remaining ham over the meat. Wrap the ham around the meat and secure with kitchen string. Peel the onions or shallots.

3 In a roasting pan, heat the oil over high heat until brown all over. Place the onions or shallots around the meat and cook until they begin to brown.

4 Add the sherry and the broth. Roast in the center of the oven for about 1 hour, basting the meat from time to time with the pan juices.

5 Remove the meat from the pan, cut into slices, and arrange with the onions on a warmed serving platter; keep warm. Return the pan juices to a boil, stirring. Add more salt and pepper, if necessary, then pour them into a sauceboat. Serve with the meat and onions.

Variation: Instead of wrapping the ham around the meat, dice it and fry in the pan with the onions.

Serrano ham

This finely veined cured ham is one of Spain's most popular delicacies, with a diversity of uses. It lends its characteristic mild flavor to a range of dishes throughout the country, north and south. It is eaten sliced or in chunks and served as a tapa with white bread; the bones are used to flavor broths and stews.

Serrano means "from the sierra" because the ham is mainly produced at an altitude of more than 2330 feet above sea level. The ham traditionally comes from the wild, black Iberian pig, which tastes best when it feeds on acorns; today, however, specially bred domestic pigs are more commonly used. The hams are buried in salt for several days or longer, then hung up to cure for anything up to a year or more in the cool, fresh air of the mountains.

Because Spanish recipes often call for diced or cubed ham, it is best to buy it in slices at least ⅛ inch thick. If serrano is unavailable, a good substitute is air-dried Italian prosciutto. Smoked hams, however, have an entirely different flavor.

Jabalí con higos en Rioja

Fairly easy • La Rioja

Wild Boar Stewed in Red Wine

Serves 4

1 medium-sized onion
2 carrots
4 garlic cloves
3 ½ oz. thick fatty bacon, sliced
1 lb. 12 oz. leg of wild boar
2 tbsp. olive oil
salt
freshly ground black pepper
2 bay leaves
1 sprig fresh, or 1 tsp. dried, thyme
1 tsp. black peppercorns
2 cloves
2 tbsp. sherry vinegar
1 cup red Rioja wine
1 cup meat broth
1 small bunch flat-leaved parsley
(about 1 oz.)
½ cup dried figs

Preparation time: 1 ½ hours

880 cal. per serving

1 Peel the onion and dice it finely. Peel the carrots and dice them finely. Peel and slice the garlic. Dice the bacon finely. Cut the boar meat into ⅜ inch dice.

2 In a flameproof casserole or heavy pan, heat the olive oil over high heat, until a haze forms over it. Add the meat, in batches if necessary, and brown. Season with salt and freshly ground pepper. Remove from the pan with a slotted spoon and reserve.

3 Fry the bacon in the oil remaining in the pan. Add the onions, carrots, and garlic and cook until the vegetables have softened.

4 Return the meat to the pan, add the bay leaves, thyme, peppercorns, cloves, and a little salt. Add the sherry vinegar and red wine, and enough broth to cover the meat. Slowly bring to a boil, cover, and simmer over low heat for about 1 hour.

5 Meanwhile, wash the parsley and shake dry. Remove the stalks and coarsely chop the leaves. Quarter the figs. About 10 minutes before the end of cooking time, stir the figs and parsley into the stew. Discard the bay leaves and cloves. Serve with potatoes.

Wine: A red Rioja is the best wine to accompany this dish, preferably the one used in the cooking.

Note: Young boar meat is the best; meat from older animals can be tough.

Cochifrita a la navarra

Fairly easy • Navarre

Lamb ragout Navarre-style

Serves 4

1 large onion
2 ¼ lb. shoulder of lamb
5 ½ oz. thick, fatty bacon
1 tbsp. olive oil
3 garlic cloves
2 tsp. mild paprika
1 sprig rosemary
salt
freshly ground black pepper
1 ¼ cups Navarre red wine
juice of ½ lemon
1 small bunch flat-leaved parsley
(about 1 oz.)

Preparation time: 1 ½ hours

380 cal. per serving

1 Peel and mince the onion. Cut the lamb into bite-sized cubes. Finely dice the bacon.

2 In a flameproof casserole or heavy pan, heat the olive oil and slowly cook the bacon until it renders up most of its fat. Add the meat, in batches if necessary, and brown on all sides.

3 Return all the meat to the pan. Stir in the onion. Peel the garlic, crush it into the pan and continue to fry for about 5 minutes, until lightly browned. Stir in the paprika, add the rosemary, and season with salt and pepper. Pour in the red wine and simmer, uncovered, until the liquid has reduced by half.

4 Stir the lemon juice into the ragout, cover, and continue to cook over low heat for about 20 minutes. Meanwhile, wash the parsley, shake dry, remove and discard the stalks, and finely chop the leaves. Discard the rosemary, check the ragout for seasoning, and stir in the parsley. Serve with potatoes and green beans.

Wine: A red wine from Navarre goes well with the ragout.

Variation:
Lamb ragout Extremadura-style
Fry the diced lamb over high heat with 1 chopped onion and 8 minced garlic cloves. Add 3 coarsely chopped beefsteak tomatoes, 2 diced bell peppers, 1 clove, and 1 bay leaf. Season with salt, pepper, cumin, and paprika. Add just enough water to cover all the ingredients, cover, and cook for about 45 minutes. Soak three slices of white bread in water and stir into the ragout. Before serving, discard the bay leaf and clove, and check the seasoning.

POULTRY AND GAME BIRDS

After fish, Spain's great love is poultry and game birds, which are combined with a wide and unusual range of ingredients, from chocolate, pine nuts, and apricots, to raisins, olives, and, of course, sherry.

Chicken is popular nationwide, and has inspired countless simple and more inventive recipes. The delicious aroma of freshly spit-roasted chicken, wafting from little booths, is a familiar one at Spain's many open-air fairs. At home, however, chicken is seldom cooked whole, but rather broiled or roasted in pieces, so that it absorbs sauces better. Sauce for chicken may made with a delicate combination of mint and orange, a robust red wine or a handful of fresh, young garlic cloves. Turkey, too, is popular, especially at Christmas; in Catalonia it is stuffed with a mixture that includes dried fruits, walnuts, pine nuts, ham or sausage, and herbs.

Thanks to its climate and topography, Spain has an abundance of game birds and it is on the main bird migration route to and from Africa. The landlocked moorland of the northeast – Aragón and Navarre – and the wooded uplands of the center, are the habitat of pheasant, partridge, and quail; wild duck and geese congregate on the extensive southern and eastern marsh lands.

Pavo a la catalana

Stuffed Roast Turkey   *Serves 6 to 8*

½ cup pitted prunes
2 tbsp. dried apricots
2 tbsp. raisins
7 tbsp. Amontillado sherry
1 oven-ready turkey, with giblets
(about 7 ½ lb.)
juice of 1 lemon
salt
freshly ground black pepper
2 oz. fatty bacon
7 oz. serrano ham
(or prosciutto if unavailable)
6 tbsp. pork dripping or good lard
6 raw butifarras
(Catalan pork sausages)
2 tart dessert apples
2 tbsp. pine nuts
4 tbsp. coarsely chopped walnuts
4 tbsp. fresh bread crumbs
1 tsp. dried thyme
1 tsp. dried oregano
1 sprig rosemary
2 bay leaves
1 ¾ cups chicken or turkey broth

**Preparation time: 2 ½ hours
(plus 1 hour marinating time)**

**1500 cal. per serving
(if serving 8)**

1 Place the prunes, apricots, and raisins in a bowl together with the sherry and leave them to soak for about 1 hour.

2 Remove the giblets from the turkey (*above*), reserve the heart and liver, and discard the rest. Rinse the turkey under cold running water, pat dry, and sprinkle inside and out with the lemon juice, salt, and pepper.

3 Preheat the oven to 425 degrees. Chop the bacon and ham into small pieces. Heat 3 tsp. of the lard in a skillet over medium heat. Squeeze the sausages out of their skins into the pan, add the ham and bacon, and sauté until lightly browned. Coarsely chop the heart and liver and add them to the pan. Continue to fry, stirring, for a further 2 minutes. Transfer to a bowl.

4 Peel, quarter, core, and slice the apples. Add the apples, pine nuts, and chopped walnuts to the bowl. Drain the prunes, apricots, and raisins, reserving the sherry, and add the fruit to the bowl. Add the bread crumbs and season with the thyme, oregano, and plenty of salt and pepper. Stir thoroughly.

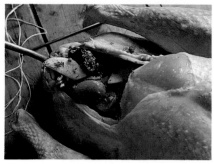

5 Stuff the turkey with the mixture, then sew up the body cavity with kitchen thread (*above*). In a large roasting pan, heat the rest of the lard. Sear the turkey in the fat over high heat for about 10 minutes, turning occasionally, until brown all over.

6 Place the turkey in the pan, breast upward. Lay the sprig of rosemary and the bay leaves over the breast, and roast in the center of the oven for about 30 minutes. Reduce the temperature to 350 degrees, pour the reserved sherry and the broth over the turkey and continue to roast for about 45 minutes, basting with the pan juices from time to time.

7 Turn off the oven and leave the turkey inside to stand for a further 25 minutes. Remove from the roasting pan and place on a serving dish. Meanwhile, cook the sauce over medium heat to reduce it, and check the seasoning. Carve the turkey, and serve with the stuffing and sauce, accompanied by potatoes and leaf spinach sprinkled, if liked, with raisins and pine nuts.

Note: This traditional Catalonian turkey recipe is a popular dish at Christmas.

Pollo con naranja y menta

Not difficult • Seville   **Chicken Breasts with Minted Orange Sauce**   *Serves 4*

2 medium-sized untreated oranges
2 tsp. olive oil
4 skinned chicken breasts
(about 7 oz. each)
salt
freshly ground black pepper
6 tsp. amontillado sherry
½ cup chicken broth
small bunch of fresh mint
(about ½ oz.)

Preparation time: 1 hour

290 cal. per serving

1 Scrub the oranges under hot running water. Thinly pare the rind from one orange, cut it into very thin strips and reserve, discarding the white parts. Cut both oranges in half crosswise. Cut one of the unpeeled halves into slices and squeeze the juice of the remaining three.

2 Heat the oil in a deep skillet over high heat and fry the chicken breasts for about 6 minutes, turning once. Transfer them to a dish, season with salt and pepper, and keep warm.

3 Drain the fat from the pan. Pour in the sherry and cook briefly, stirring to dislodge any residues in the pan. Add the strips of orange peel and juice, and the broth. Cook the sauce over high heat until reduced by about one third.

4 Rinse the mint under cold running water and shake dry. Reserve a few small sprigs for decoration, and tear off the rest of the leaves. Finely chop the leaves and stir them into the sauce. Season with salt and pepper. Place the chicken breasts in the sauce, cover the pan, and simmer for about 10 minutes until cooked through.

5 Arrange the chicken on a serving dish. Pour the sauce over it, and garnish with the mint sprigs and orange slices. Serve, if you like, on a bed of saffron rice (see page 105, Note).

Wine: A rosé from Catalonia is a good accompaniment to this dish.

Sherry

This famous wine, one of the world's oldest, derives its name from the Andalusian city of Jerez de la Frontera, in southwest Spain. It owes the distinctive flavor and fine quality to the region's chalky soil, exceptional climate and a form of yeast, known as flor and unique to Jerez, that aids fermentation.

The traditional method by which sherry is matured and blended is known as the solera system. The solera comprises anything from 20 to 100 kegs, stacked in tiers up to five rows high. The youngest sherries are at the top; the oldest, dating from the 19th century, are at the bottom. When the fully matured sherry is drawn off at the bottom, the barrel is filled from the one above, and so on, up the stack until space is left in the top barrel for the new year's wine. In this way, the sherry is continually blended, thus eliminating vintages and maintaining a consistently high quality

There are four basic types of sherry, the driest being the pale fino and manzanilla, best drunk chilled as an aperitif. The darker amontillado is less dry, but also suitable before a meal. The deep amber oloroso and cream sherries, served at room temperature, are an ideal choice to accompany desserts.

Pollo a la campesina
Country-style chicken

Not difficult • Aragón

Serves 4

1 ¼ lb. beefsteak tomatoes
2 large red bell peppers
(about 12 oz.)
1 oven-ready chicken (about 3 lb.)
3 tsp. olive oil
salt • freshly ground black pepper
1 tsp. medium-hot paprika
4 garlic cloves
1 cup dry white wine
1 small dried chili pepper
(see Glossary)
1 sprig thyme • 1 bay leaf
4 tbsp. olives, stuffed with
pimientos

Preparation time: 1 ½ hours

600 cal. per serving

1 Preheat the oven to 475 degrees. Plunge the tomatoes briefly in boiling water, skin and cut into eighths. Skin the bell peppers (page 34, top recipe, Step 1), then halve, remove the stalks, seeds and ribs, and cut the flesh into strips. Reduce oven temperature to 350 degrees.

2 Divide the chicken into 8 pieces. Heat the oil in a flameproof casserole over medium heat. Add the chicken pieces and fry until lightly browned. Season with salt, pepper, and the paprika. Peel the garlic, crush the flesh, and add to the casserole.

3 Pour over the wine, and add the chili pepper, thyme, bay leaf, tomatoes, and sweet peppers. Cover the casserole, and cook in the center of the oven for about 50 minutes.

4 About 10 minutes before the end of the cooking time, slice the olives and stir them into the casserole. Serve the chicken straight from the casserole, with crusty white bread.

Wine: A dry white wine goes best with the dish.

Note: If you prefer, buy 8 chicken servings or ask your butcher to cut the chicken for you.

Pollo al ajillo
Garlic Chicken

Not difficult • Many regions

Serves 4

1 oven-ready chicken (about 3
lb. 5 oz.)
1 garlic head
5 tsp. olive oil
salt
freshly ground black pepper
1 tsp. medium-hot paprika
1 cup dry white wine
2 bay leaves
1 small bunch flat-leaved parsley
(about 1 oz.)

Preparation time: about 1 hour

670 cal. per serving

1 Preheat the oven to 350 degrees. Divide the chicken into 8 pieces. Break off the garlic cloves, peel and slice them.

2 Heat the oil in a flameproof casserole over medium heat and fry the chicken pieces, in 2 batches if necessary, until lightly browned. Season with salt, pepper, and the paprika, then remove and keep warm.

3 Add the garlic to the remaining fat in the casserole and sauté over low heat, until softened. Add the wine and the bay leaves and bring to a boil.

4 Return the chicken pieces to the casserole, cover, and cook in the center of the oven for about 40 minutes. Meanwhile, wash the parsley, shake it dry, and chop it fairly coarsely. Serve the chicken straight from the casserole, sprinkled with the parsley and accompanied by crusty white bread – good for mopping up the garlic sauce.

Wine: A dry white wine from Galicia, such as Albariño, goes particularly well with the dish.

Note: The dish is best cooked with young, fresh garlic.

Pollo a la vasca

Fairly easy • Basque Country **Chicken Casserole Basque-style** *Serves 4*

1 ¼ cups shallots
2 large red bell peppers
(about 12 oz.)
3 ½ oz. serrano ham
(or prosciutto if unavailable)
4 medium-sized green bell peppers
4 garlic cloves
1 oven-ready chicken (about 2½ lb.)
3 tbsp. pork dripping or lard
salt
freshly ground black pepper
4 tbsp. tomato paste
1 cup dry white wine

Preparation time: 1 ½ hours

690 cal. per serving

1 Preheat the oven to 475 degrees. Peel the shallots. Skin the red peppers (page 34, top recipe. Step 1). Reduce the oven temperature to 350 degrees. Halve the red peppers, remove the seeds and ribs, and cut the flesh into narrow strips.

2 Dice the ham. Wash the green peppers, remove the stalks, seeds and ribs, and cut into narrow strips. Peel the garlic.

3 Divide the chicken into 8 pieces. Heat the dripping or lard in a flameproof casserole, and fry chicken pieces over medium heat until lightly browned. Season with salt and pepper, remove from the pan and keep warm.

4 Fry the shallots in the remaining fat until lightly browned. Stir in the diced ham and the tomato paste. Crush the garlic and add to the casserole. Add the wine and the red and green peppers. Arrange the chicken pieces on the bed of vegetables, cover, and bake in the oven for about 50 minutes. Serve with potatoes.

Wine: a dry white Rioja is excellent with this dish.

Pintada con albaricoques

Guinea Fowl with Apricots

More complex • Catalonia   *Serves 4*

*1 large onion • 2 carrots
2 small oven-ready guinea-fowl
(about 1 lb. 4 oz. each)
salt
freshly ground black pepper
3 tbsp. olive oil • 2 garlic cloves
3 tbsp. Spanish brandy
2-inch piece cinnamon stick
2 bay leaves
1 sprig fresh, or 1 tsp. dried thyme
1 small bunch flat-leaved parsley
(about 1 oz.)
1 ¾ cups chicken broth
1 ¼ cups fresh, or 1 ¾ cups dried,
apricots
4 tbsp. pine nuts
1 to 2 tsp. red wine vinegar*

Preparation time: 1 ½ hours

400 cal. per serving

1 Peel and mince the onion. Peel and slice the carrots. Season the guinea fowl inside and out with salt and pepper, and truss them with kitchen twine (see Glossary)

2 Preheat the oven to 350 degrees. Heat the oil in a flameproof casserole over medium heat and fry the guinea fowl until lightly browned. Add the onion and the carrots and sauté for about 5 minutes. Peel the garlic, crush the flesh, and add it to the pan.

3 Pour over the brandy, and add the cinnamon stick, bay leaves, thyme, and parsley. Pour on the broth, cover the casserole, and roast in the center of the oven for about 30 minutes.

4 If using fresh apricots, plunge them briefly in boiling water, rinse with ice-cold water, then peel and stone. After the guinea fowl have been in the oven for about 30 minutes, add the apricots (fresh or dried.) Return to the oven and cook for a further 25 minutes. Meanwhile, in a dry skillet, toast the pine nuts until golden-brown.

5 Remove the guinea fowl from the casserole and keep warm. Discard the bay leaves, cinnamon stick, fresh thyme, if using, and parsley. Purée the sauce in a food processor, return to the casserole and reduce to thicken. Season with salt, pepper, and the vinegar.

6 Untruss the guinea fowl. Carve and arrange on a serving dish, and sprinkle with the pine nuts. Serve, accompanied by rice and the sauce.

Pato a la sevillana

Takes a little time • Seville

Roast Duck with Orange and Olive Sauce

Serves 4

1 oven-ready duck (about 4 lb.)
salt
freshly ground black pepper
1 large onion
4 garlic cloves
2 carrots
1 untreated orange
3 tbsp. olive oil
1 tbsp. all-purpose flour
1 bay leaf
1 small dried chili pepper
1 cup dry white wine
¾ cup pitted green olives
sugar
1 tbsp. white wine vinegar

Preparation time: 2 hours

1300 cal. per serving

1 Preheat the oven to 475 degrees. Rinse the duck under cold water and pat dry. Season it inside and out with salt and pepper (*see above*).

2 Peel and mince the onion and the garlic. Peel and slice the carrots. Scrub the orange under hot running water, then cut into slices crosswise.

3 Heat the oil in a roasting pan or large, shallow flameproof casserole over medium heat. Add the duck and fry it on all sides until brown all over. Add the onion, garlic, and carrots to the pan, and sauté briefly. Stir in the all-purpose flour. Add the bay leaf, chili pepper, and orange slices.

4 Place in the center of the oven and roast the duck for about 20 minutes. Reduce the oven temperature to 400 degrees, pour over the wine, and cook for a further 45 to 50 minutes, or until done.

5 Remove the duck from the pan and turn off the oven. Place the duck on a rack in another pan and leave to stand in the cooling oven for about 15 minutes. Meanwhile slice the olives.

6 Remove the bay leaf, chili, and the orange slices from the roasting pan, and, over medium heat, reduce the sauce by one third. Season with salt, pepper, a little sugar, and the wine vinegar. Sprinkle the olives into the sauce, and heat through.

7 Carve the duck into serving pieces (*above*) and arrange on a warmed dish. Serve accompanied by the sauce and boiled potatoes.

Wine: A full-bodied red wine, such as a Rioja, goes well with this dish.

Variation: Instead of oranges and olives, use 6 to 8 fresh figs cut into quarters. Or, cook the duck with a quince paste or jelly, which gives it a really distinctive flavor.

Note: The dish is traditionally cooked with bitter Seville oranges, usually available between the end of December and early February. If you are cooking for only two people, it is easier to buy ready prepared duck breasts.

Codornices emborrachados

Quail in Wine and Brandy sauce

Needs a little care • Castille

Serves 2 to 4

4 oven-ready quail
(about 10½ oz. each)
1 medium-sized onion
2 oz. serrano ham
(or prosciutto if unavailable)
4 tbsp. olive oil
salt
freshly ground black pepper
3 tbsp. Spanish brandy
1 cup dry white wine
7 tbsp. heavy cream

Preparation time: 1 hour

(if serving 4)
710 cal. per serving

1 Cut the quail in half lengthwise. Finely chop the onion. Dice the ham.

2 Heat the oil in a flameproof casserole or sauté pan over medium heat and lightly brown the quail on both sides. Remove from the pan and season with salt and pepper.

3 Add the onion and the ham to the remaining fat, and sauté over low heat for about 3 minutes. Add the brandy and the wine and bring to a boil.

4 Return the quail to the pan, cover and cook over low heat for about 30 minutes. Transfer the quail to a serving dish and keep warm. Add the cream to the sauce, then continue to cook, uncovered, until reduced by about a third. Season with salt and pepper. Pour the sauce over the quail, and serve, accompanied by rice or potatoes.

Variation: Quail in chocolate sauce
Fry the halved quail in oil until golden-brown, season, remove from the pan and keep warm. Sauté 1 chopped onion and 2 chopped garlic cloves until soft. Add 1 cup red wine, cover, and simmer for about 15 minutes. Return the quail to the pan and simmer for about 8 minutes. Remove the quail and keep warm. Stir 3 tbsp. red vine vinegar and 3 tbsp. grated unsweetened chocolate into the pan liquid. Heat through slowly until the chocolate melts and the sauce thickens. Pour over the quail and serve.

Pichones a la toledana

Toledo-style Squab

Fairly easy • Toledo

Serves 4

2 onions
5 garlic cloves
4 oven-ready squab (about 10 ½ oz.)
4 tbsp. olive oil
salt
freshly ground black pepper
6 tbsp. dry sherry
1 tbsp. sherry vinegar

Preparation time: 1 ½ hours

690 cal. per serving

1 Peel and finely chop the onions. Leave the garlic cloves unpeeled, but lightly crush them with the back of a spoon.

2 Divide the squab into quarters. Heat the oil in a flameproof casserole over medium heat and brown the squab pieces. Season with salt and pepper. Add the onions and garlic, then the sherry and vinegar. Cover, and cook over low heat for about 40 minutes, adding a little water if too dry.

3 Remove the meat from the casserole and keep warm. Cook over high heat for about 3 minutes, to reduce the sauce.

Check the seasoning and adjust if necessary, then strain the sauce. Serve the squab, accompanied by the sauce and crusty white bread.

Drink: A dry fino sherry goes particularly well with this dish.

Variation: To make a more substantial version of this dish, you can add the coarsely chopped flesh of 3 skinned, deseeded beefsteak tomatoes and 4 tbsp. pitted green olives.

Note: You can substitute dry white wine for the sherry, in which case serve the same white wine with the meal.

DESSERTS AND PASTRIES

With a year-round assortment of delicious produce from which to choose, one of the Spaniards' favorite ways of rounding off a meal is with fresh fruits. In spring, it is a bowl of sweet strawberries from Catalonia; on a hot August day, a slice of ice-cold melon from Murcia and in December, a juicy, freshly picked orange from Valencia.

In addition to its store of natural riches, Spain also boasts a variety of enticing desserts. The culinary influence of the Moors pervades much of the cuisine, nowhere more so than in sweets and candies, where much use is made of egg yolks, honey, and almonds. Marzipan is of Moorish origin, as is *turrón*, the famous Jijona, and Alicante nougat.

In the days when egg whites were widely used to clarify sherry, the leftover yolks were donated to convents, where the nuns transformed them into a variety of exquisite candies such as yemas, candied yolks, or *Tocino de cielo*, a rich caramel custard made from only sugar and egg yolks. Today, continuing the centuries-old tradition, many people in Andalusia still order desserts, candies, and pastries from their local convent for festivities at Christmas or Easter, or to celebrate saints' days.

Torta de almendras

Not difficult • Andalucía

Almond Tart

Serves 8 to 12

For the pastry:
1 ¾ cups all-purpose flour
⅓ cup butter
4 tbsp. sugar
1 egg
1 tbsp. milk
For the filling:
⅔ cup almonds
4 eggs
4 tbsp. sugar
4 tbsp. cream sherry
granted rind of 1 untreated lemon
salt

Preparation time: 1 ½ hours

310 cal. per serving
(if serving 12)

1 Sift the all-purpose flour into a bowl and make a well in the center. Dice the butter and add it to the well, together with the sugar. Rub together with your fingers until the mixture has a coarse, mealy texture. Make another well, add the egg and the milk, and stir with a knife until the mixture coheres. Gently knead the dough into a ball, wrap in foil or plastic wrap, and chill for about 30 minutes.

2 For the filling, blanch the almonds (page 50, Step 1), pat them dry, and grind finely in a food processor or in a mortar with a pestle. Separate the eggs and reserve the whites. Whisk the yolks together with the sugar until frothy. Stir in the ground almonds, sherry, and the grated lemon rind.

3 Preheat the oven to 425 degrees. Whisk the egg whites and a little salt until the whites form stiff peaks. Fold the egg whites evenly into the egg-and-almond mixture.

4 Grease a 10-inch springform pan or pie pan. On an all-purpose floured work surface, roll out the pastry. Carefully line the pan with the pastry, making the rim about 1 inch high. fill the case with the almond paste and level the surface.

5 Bake in the center of the oven for about 30 minutes. If the top begins to brown too quickly, cover it with aluminum foil. Remove the tart from the oven and leave to cool on a wire rack. Serve with cream if you like.

Almonds

The almond is the edible seed of a small fruit closely related to the plum and the peach. Almonds are native to Asia and were first cultivated in Europe by the Greeks; they were introduced to Spain by the Moors. Spain is now among the world's leading exporters of almonds; the lovely almond trees – which are covered in a mass of white blossoms early in the year before most other flowers emerge – are a familiar sight.

There are two basic types of almond: the sweet, edible variety, which contains 50 to 60 percent oil; and the bitter variety – never eaten raw – whose essential oil is used in the manufacture of flavoring extracts.

Almonds can be bough unpeeled, blanched, chopped, flaked or ground. Where a recipe calls for blanched almonds, it is better to buy unpeeled ones and blanch them yourself, because the almonds' thin brown skin preserves the freshness and flavor.

Raw or cooked, almonds are very popular in Spanish cuisine, lending a distinctive flavor to soups, sauces, seafood dishes, pastries and the famous nougat, turrón.

Flao

Fairly easy • Ibiza

Spanish Cheesecake

Serves 8 to 12

1 ¼ cups all-purpose flour
salt
4 tbsp. Spanish anis, or other
aniseed-flavored liqueur
4 tbsp. olive oil
4 eggs • ¾ cup sugar
1 ¾ cups cream cheese or farmer
cheese
1 small bunch fresh mint
(about 1 oz.)
powdered sugar for dusting

Preparation time: 1 hour 10 minutes

310 cal. per serving
(if serving 12)

1 Sift the all-purpose flour into a bowl. Add the salt, liqueur, olive oil, and 4 tbsp. water and mix together. Knead into a smooth dough and shape into a ball. Cover and leave to stand for about 30 minutes in a cool place.

2 Meanwhile, whisk together the eggs and sugar, until creamy. Mash the cheese thoroughly with a fork, then stir into the eggs and sugar with the whisk.

3 Preheat the oven to 425 degrees. Wash the mint and pat it dry. Tear off the leaves, chop them coarsely, and stir into the filling.

4 Grease a 10-inch springform or cheesecake pan. Roll the pastry out thinly and line the tin, making an edge about 4 cm high. Pour the filling into the case and level the surface.

5 Bake in the center of the oven for 30 to 40 minutes, until set. When cooked, leave the cheesecake to cool on a wire cooling rack. Before serving, dust with a little sifted powdered sugar.

Note: In Ibiza, this cheesecake is traditionally made with fresh, white ewe's-milk cheese.

Turrón de Jijona

Fairly easy • Alicante

Almond Nougat

Makes about 25 slices

5 ½ cups almonds
3 ½ cups powdered sugar
½ cup clear honey
2 egg whites

Preparation time: 20 minutes
(plus 1 week drying time)

230 cal. per slice

1 Blanch the almonds (page 50, Step 1) and wipe them dry. In a dry skillet, toast the almonds until golden, stirring constantly. Set aside about ¾ cup almonds and finely grind the remainder.

2 Reserve 20 whole almonds and place the rest in a bowl together with the ground almonds and the powdered (confectioners') sugar. Add the honey, then the egg whites, and stir thoroughly to form a thick paste.

3 Shape the almond paste into bars about 2 inches wide and 8 inches long. Lay the bars on a sheet of nonstick baking paper, decorate with the reserved whole almonds, and leave in a cool place for about 1 week to dry.

4 Cut the nougat into slices and serve.

Note: This celebrated nougat, traditionally a Christmas candy, is delicious served with coffee after a meal, or simply as a snack. Be sure to use fresh eggs from a source you trust for this recipe, as raw eggs can contain the salmonella bacteria that causes food poisoning.

Leche frita

Custard Fritters

Takes time • Many regions

Makes 18 squares or 36 triangles

4 eggs
⅔ cup butter
2 cups all-purpose flour
½ cup sugar
1 cup milk
2-inch piece cinnamon stick
1 piece untreated lemon rind
1 piece untreated orange rind
¾ cup fresh fine bread crumbs
8 tbsp. olive oil
powdered sugar
ground cinnamon

Preparation time: 50 minutes
(plus cooling time)

240 cal. per square
120 cal. per triangle

1 Separate the eggs; reserve the whites in the refrigerator. Slowly melt the butter in a heavy saucepan. Stir in 1 ¾ cups of the all-purpose flour, bring to a boil, and stir in the sugar.

2 In another saucepan, heat the milk together with the cinnamon stick, lemon and orange rind. Bring to a boil, then stir into the flour mixture.

3 Remove the pan from the heat and discard the cinnamon stick and the lemon and orange rind. Using a hand whisk, beat in the egg yolks one by one.

4 Oil a rectangular dish, about 12 by 6 inches. Fill with the custard to a depth of about 1 inch. Refrigerate for at least 3 hours or until set, preferably overnight.

5 When set, cut the custard into 2-inch squares, or halve again into triangles. Whisk the egg whites. Dip the custard pieces in the remaining flour, then in the beaten egg whites, and coat with the bread crumbs.

6 Heat the oil in a skillet over medium heat and fry the coated custard pieces on both sides until golden-brown. Arrange on a serving dish, sprinkle with powdered sugar and ground cinnamon, and serve warm or cold.

Note: These fritters are an ideal accompaniment to a compote of berries or other fruit.

Churros
Spanish Donuts

A little more complex • Many regions

Makes about 30 donuts

salt
2 ½ cups all-purpose flour
olive, or other, oil for deep frying
powdered sugar for dusting

Preparation time: 45 minutes
(plus 10 minutes standing time)

290 cal. per churro

1 Bring 2 cups salted water to a boil in a heavy saucepan.

2 Reduce the heat to low, add the all-purpose flour, and stir vigorously with a wooden spoon until the dough forms a ball. Remove from the heat, cover, and leave to stand for about 10 minutes.

3 Heat the oil in a deep pan until it sizzles when a small piece of the dough is dropped in. Transfer the dough to a large piping bag fitted with a wide star nozzle. Squeeze rings of the dough, a few at a time, into the hot oil. Fry until just golden, remove with a slotted spoon, and drain on kitchen paper. Repeat until all the dough has been used.

4 Serve immediately, dusted with a little powdered sugar.

Note: These little fritters, freshly fried, can be bought from stands at any fair or festival in Spain, and are sold by the bag in special churrería stores. They are delicious eaten for breakfast, or as a snack after late-night festivities, with thick, hot chocolate. They can also be served as dessert.

Crema catalana
Catalan Caramel Cream

A little more complex • Catalonia

Serves 4

2 cups milk
1 vanilla pod
2-inch piece cinnamon stick
2 eggs
4 egg yolks
sugar
For the caramel topping:
½ cup sugar

Preparation time: 50 minutes
(plus 1 ½ hour chilling time)

360 cal. per serving

1 Pour the milk into a saucepan. Slit open the vanilla pod, scrape out the seeds, and add them with the vanilla pod to the milk. Add a cinnamon stick, then bring the milk slowly to a boil. Remove the pan from the heat.

2 Place the eggs and the egg yolks in a bowl with the sugar and whisk for 10 to 15 minutes, or until pale yellow and creamy.

3 Remove the vanilla pod and the cinnamon stick from the milk. Trickle the milk slowly into the egg mixture, stirring constantly (*above*).

4 Place the bowl in a large pan filled with simmering water and whisk for about 15 minutes, until the custard thickens.

5 Pour the custard into four individual dishes. leave to cool, then refrigerate for about 30 minutes.

6 To make the caramel topping, place the sugar in a saucepan with ½ cup water, and simmer over very low heat until it caramelizes but is still liquid. Spoon the hot caramel over the chilled custards (*above*); it will cool to form a firm layer. Return to the refrigerator, and serve well chilled.

Variation: Catalan cream and pears
Make the cream as above but omit the caramel topping. Preheat the oven to 400 degrees. Peel, halve, and core one pear per person. Place the pears in a baking dish with the juice of 1 medium-sized orange, ¾ cup Malaga or medium-sweet sherry, 4 tbsp. raisins, 4 tbsp. chopped almonds and 2 cloves. Bake it in the center of the oven for about 30 minutes. Serve warm or chilled, accompanied by the custard.

Tocino de cielo

"Bacon from Heaven"

Serves 4

½ *cup sugar*
8 egg yolks
grated rind of 1 untreated lemon
almond oil

Preparation time: 20 minutes
(plus 30 minutes or more chilling time)

260 cal. per serving

1 In a small saucepan, dissolve the sugar in 1 ½ cup water over low heat, stirring, then increase the heat and boil without stirring for about 1 minute to form a thick syrup. Remove from the heat.

2 Whisk the egg yolks and stir them slowly into the sugar syrup, then strain the mixture through a fine sieve. Add the grated lemon rind.

3 Grease 4 custard cups, or one large bowl, with a little almond oil, then fill with them the mixture.

4 Stand the custard cups in a large, deep pan. Add boiling water to about two-thirds of the depth of the custard cups and cover them with a lid or a sheet of nonstick baking paper. Cook over medium heat for about 10 minutes, then test the custards by gently pressing with your finger – they should feel springy. If not yet set, cook for a few minutes more.

5 Let the custards cool before unmolding them. chill for at least 30 minutes, longer if possible, before serving.

Note: Tocino de cielo though similar to Crema catalana and the French crème caramel, is made without milk. The streaky appearance is why it is called "bacon."

Bollos de cuajada

Cottage cheese balls

Serves 4 to 6

2 cups cottage cheese or quark
4 eggs
1 tbsp. ground cinnamon
grated rind of 1 untreated lemon
4 heaping tbsp. all-purpose flour
olive or corn oil for deep frying
6 tbsp. clear honey

Preparation time: 30 minutes
(plus 10 minutes standing time)

230 cal. per serving
(if serving 6)

1 Thoroughly drain the cottage cheese or quark and mash it with a fork.

2 Whisk the eggs in a bowl. Add the cinnamon, grated lemon rind, and cheese or quark and work into a thick dough. Sprinkle in half the flour. Cover the bowl and leave the dough to stand for about 10 minutes.

3 With floured hands (using the remaining flour), shape the dough into little balls about the size of walnuts. Heat a generous amount of oil in a deep skillet over medium heat, and deep-fry the balls until golden-brown. Remove them with a slotted spoon and drain on kitchen paper.

4 Arrange the cheese balls on a warmed serving dish, pour the honey over them and serve immediately.

Note: In the Canary Islands, these delicious little cakes are traditionally eaten during the carnival season.

Suggested Menus

Spanish cuisine is enormously versatile; restaurant menus are arranged not by course but, as in this book, by category, allowing you to create a meal to suit your own taste and budget. When planning a menu, bear in mind that many of the tapas, and the rice, egg, or vegetable dishes, make excellent, inexpensive meals. This selection, compiled from recipes featured in the book, contains suggestions to suit every occasion from simple, everyday meals to more elaborate ones suitable for festive occasions. For a tapas party, choose a selection of dishes from page 32 through 47 adding, say, serrano ham, Manchego cheese, olives, pistachio nuts, or salted almonds, and serve with white bread and chilled sherry.

Everyday menus

Summer Salad (Pipirrana)	38
Garlic Chicken (Pollo al ajillo)	118
Peaches Poached in Red Wine*	—
Shrimp Omelet (Tortilla de gambas)	40
Roast Loin of Pork Málaga-style (Solomillo a la malagueña)	101
Saffron Rice (see Note, page 105) and vegetables	—
Almond Tart (Torta de almendras)	128
Almond and Saffron Soup (Sopa de almendras)	50
Trout Stuffed with Ham (Truchas a la navarra)	93
Spinach with Almonds and Raisins (Espinacas Sacromonte)	68
Fruit Salad*	—

When time is short

Garlic Soup (Sopa de ajo)	53
Chicken Breasts with Minted Orange Sauce (Pollo con naranja y menta)	116
Selection of Fresh Fruit*	—
Chilled Grape and Almond Soup (Ajo blanco con uvas)	58
Flamenco Eggs (Huevos a la flamenca)	79
Ice Cream, or Manchego Cheese with Quince Jelly*	—
Garlic Shrimp (Gambas al ajillo)	42
Hake with Caper Sauce (Merluza con alcaparras)	88
Green Salad*	—
Pears Poached in White Wine*	
Chicken in Sherry (Pechuga de pollo en jerez)	44
Gilt-head Bream in a Salt Crust (Dorada al sal)	90
Fried Bananas*	

Mixed Pepper Omelet (Piperrada)	78
Baked Scallops (Vieiras a la gallega)	84
Ice cream with Fruits	—

Menus for hot summer days

Cold Vegetable Soup (Gazpacho)	58
Calf's Tongue with Pomegranate Sauce (Lenguas con salsa de granada)	105
Rice with pine nuts and Raisins*	—
Fruit Sorbet*	—
Marinated Anchovies (Boquerones en vinagre)	47
Garlic Soup (Vieiras a la gallega)	84
Cold Rice Pudding*	—
Russian Salad (Ensaladilla rusa)	40
Fish Soup (Caldo de pescado)	55
Guinea Fowl with Apricots (Pintada con albaricoques)	121
Cheese and Fresh Fruit*	—
Chilled Grape and Almond soup (Ajo blanco con uvas)	58
Chicken Breasts with Minted Orange Sauce (Pollo con naranja y menta)	116
Vanilla Ice Cream*, topped with Crumbled Almond Nougat (Turrón de Jijona)	131
Carrot Salad (Ensalada de zanahoria)	37
Garlic Shrimp (Gambas al ajillo) – double the quantities given in recipe	42
Honeydew Melon with Cream Sherry*	—

Cold-weather menus

Chicken Croquettes (Croquetas de pollo)	37
Stewed Tripe with Chorizo (Callos a la gallega)	56
Almond Tart (Torta de almendras)	128
Baked Zucchini (Calabacines al horno)	74
Stuffed Mushrooms (Champiñones rellenos)	45
Lentil Casserole (Cazuela de lentejas)	53
Catalan Caramel Cream (Crema catalana)	134
Kidneys in Sherry (Riñones al jerez)	34
Russian Salad (Ensaladilla rusa)	40
Chickpea and Spinach Stew (Potaje de garbanzos)	60
Almond Nougat (Turrón de Jijona)	131
Fish Soup (Caldo de pescado)	55
Pork Loin with Ham (Solomillo de cerdo con jamón)	108
Vegetable Ragout (Pisto manchego)	68
Fresh Oranges*	—

Menus to prepare in advance

Pearl Onions in Sherry Vinegar (Cebolletas al vinagre de jerez)	33
Moorish-style Kabobs (Pinchos morunos)	39
Lentil Casserole (Cazuela de lentejas)	53
Custard Fritters (Leche frita)	132
Vegetable Ragout (Pisto manchego)	68
Country-style Chicken (Pollo a la campesina)	118
Catalan Caramel Cream (Crema catalana)	134
Baked Zucchini (Calabacines al horno)	74
Potato Omelet (Tortilla de patatas)	76
Baked Sea-bream (Besugo al horno)	86
Vanilla Ice Cream with Fresh Figs*	—
Almond and Saffron Soup (Sopa de almendras)	50
Braised Oxtail Seville-style (Rabo de toro a la sevillana)	102
Fruit Sorbet*	—
Marinated Anchovies (Boquerones en vinagre)	47
Veal and Vegetable Casserole (Ternera "La Mancha")	98
Cheesecake (Flao)	131

Vegetarian menus

Russian Salad (Ensaladilla rusa)	40
Chickpea and Spinach Stew (Potaje de garbanzos)	60
Eggplant Alpujarra-style (Berenjenas Alpujarra)	72
Fried Artichokes (Alcachofas fritas)	67
Fresh Fruit or Cheese*	—
Summer Salad (Pipirrana)	38
Potato Omelet (Torilla de patatas)	76
Baked Mixed Vegetables (Escalivada)	70
Cheesecake (Flao)	131
Rye Bread with Tomatoes and Olives*	—
Spinach with Almonds and Raisins (Espinacas Sacromonte) served with rice	68
Cottage Cheese Balls (Bollos de cuajada)	136
Marinated Red Peppers (Pimientos en adobo)	34
Cold Vegetable soup (Gazpacho)	58
Baked Zucchini (Calabacines al horno)	74
Apples with Sweet Sherry or Dessert Wine*	—

Fish and Seafood menus

Garlic Shrimp (Gambas al ajillo)	42
Summer Salad (Pipirrana)	38
Shellfish Stew (Zarzuela de mariscos)	82
Almond Tart (Torta de almendras)	128
Marinated Anchovies (Bouquerones en vinagre)	47
Clams Fisherman-style (Almejas a la marinera)	94
Salt Cod in Olive Oil and Garlic Sauce (Bacalao al pil-pil)	93
Baked Mixed Vegetables (Escalivada)	70
Catalan Caramel Cream (Crema catalana)	134
Marinated Red Peppers (Pimientos en adobo)	34
Shrimp Omelet (Tortilla de gambas)	40
Fish Soup (Caldo de pescado)	55
Baked Scallops (Vieiras a la gallega)	84
Lemon Sorbet*	—

Menus for Entertaining

Meatballs in Tomato Sauce (Albóndigas en salsa de tomate)	32
Garlic Soup (Sopa de ajo)	53
Chicken and Seafood Rice (Paella)	64
Catalan Caramel Cream (Crema catalana)	134
Chilled Grape and Almond Soup (Ajo blanco con uvas)	58
Quail in Wine and Brandy Sauce (Codornices emborrachados) – half quail per person as appetizer	125
Gilt-head Bream in a Salt Crust (Dorada al sal)	90
Mixed Pepper Omelet (Piperrada)	78
Cottage Cheese Balls (Bollos de cuajada)	136
Tapas with Apéritifs:	
Chicken Croquettes (Croquetas de pollo)	37
Shrimp Omelet (Tortilla de gambas)	40
Marinated Red Peppers (Pimientos en adobo)	34
Olives and Salted Almonds*	—
Almond and Saffron Soup (Sopa de almendras)	50
Salmon with Ham and Cider Sauce (Salmón a la ribereña)	86
Toledo-style Squab (Pichones a la toledana)	125
Mixed Salad*	—
"Bacon from Heaven" (Tocino de cielo)	136

Christmas

Fish Soup (Caldo de pescado)	55
Baked Sea-bream (Besugo al horno)	86
Stuffed Roast Turkey (Pavo a la catalana) – served with red cabbage or leaf spinach	114
Almond Nougat (Turrón de Jijona)	131
and/or Marzipan and other Christmas candies*	—
Coffee and Anis liqueur or brandy*	

* Indicates either simple dishes such as green salad or poached fruits, for which no recipes or page reference is indicated, or items such as nougat or sorbet, which can be obtained from supermarkets or specialist delicatessens.

Glossary

This glossary is intended as a brief guide to some less familiar cookery terms and ingredients, including words and items found on Spanish menus.

Aceite, acette de oliva: oil, olive oil

Aceitunas: olives (see page 71)

Ajo: garlic (see page 42)

Aioli: garlic mayonnaise made from garlic, olive oil, egg yolks, and lemon juice. Delicious served with broiled fish or meat, with potatoes or coarse rye bread.

Albóndigas: small meatballs made from ground meats, fish, or chicken, usually served in a sauce as tapas

Alcachofa: artichoke

Alcaparra: caper

Almejas: clams. Mainly farmed in Galicia, and often served in a white wine sauce.

Almendra: almond (see page 128)

Amontillado: medium-dry sherry, amber-colored and full-bodied. Less dry than a fino sherry. It can be drunk chilled before a meal.

Angulas: silvery, mild-flavored elvers, often served in a garlic sauce.

Anís: Spanish aniseed-flavored liqueur

Arroz: rice. The starchy round-grained rice produced in the Levante, around Valencia, is the principal ingredient of paella and many other Spanish rice dishes. Italian aborio or vialone rice or Carolina rice can be used instead.

Azafrán: saffron (see page 50)

Bacalao: dried salt cod. A Spanish favorite, especially in the north and inland, salt cod has a strong flavor and should soaked for 24 to 36 hours before cooking, to soften it and remove the salt.

Berenjena: eggplant

Besugo: sea-bream. Found both in the Atlantic and the Mediterranean, it has firm, white flesh, and is often baked whole, either stuffed or in a sauce.

Blanch: to plunge food into boiling water for a short period. Done for a number of reasons: to facilitate skinning foods such as tomatoes, peaches, or almonds; to remove strong flavors; or to soften vegetables before cooking.

Bocadillo: savory bread-roll or sandwich

Boquerón: fresh anchovy. These little fish are usually served marinated or deep-fried, but can also be broiled, grilled or barbecued.

Café con leche, café solo: coffee with milk, small black coffee

Callos: tripe (menudo)

Caramelize: to heat sugar, or a food naturally rich in sugar, such as fruit, until the sugar turns brown and syrupy

Catalan-style: usually indicates a dish prepared with chocolate, nuts, or sausage

Cava: Spanish sparkling wine produced by the méthode champenoise; the best cavas make a good alternative to champagne.

Cebolla: onion

Cerdo: pork

Champiñones: mushrooms

Chili peppers: a variety of hot red or green peppers. They contain volatile oils that can irritate the skin and eyes and must be handled with caution. Wash hands immediately after using them. The seeds of the chili are the hottest part; this should be taken into account when using fresh or dried chili peppers.

Chorizo: strongly spiced paprika sausage (see page 56)

Chuleta: chop or cutlet

Churros: small ridged, piped donuts traditionally served for breakfast

Comino: cumin. Brought to Spain by the Moors, this spice is appreciated especially in southern Spain for its unmistakable tangy taste. Cumin is available as whole seeds or powdered

Cream sherry: full-bodied, sweet, heavy dessert wine

Dulce: dessert or candy

Ensalada: salad, usually simply dressed with olive oil and sherry vinegar

Espinacas: spinach, traditionally served in Spain with raisins and pine nuts

Estofado: stew

Fabada: white bean and pork stew, the most famous version of which comes from Asturias

Fino: dry sherry, light and pale yellow in color. Serve chilled as an aperitif or to accompany an appetizer.

Fresa: strawberry. The first strawberries grown in the Huelva area appear on the market as early as mid-February.

Frito, frita: fried. In Spain, olive oil is most frequently used for frying.

Fruta: fruit. Spain boasts a great variety of fresh fruit; more exotic varieties such as bananas and pineapples grow in the Canary Islands.

Gambas: shrimp

Garbanzo: chickpea, a popular pulse used in stews and salads

Gazpacho: Cold, refreshing vegetable soup, popular in the summer months; the tomato-and-garlic version from Andalusia is the best known.

Granada: pomegranate. If the fruit is fresh, the chewy seeds are good enough to eat. Pulp and juice are added to fruit salads, or used to make drinks or sorbets.

Helado: ice cream

Hígado: liver

Higo: fig. Fresh or dried figs are often served with ham, and are also popular as a dessert.

Al horno: baked or roasted in the oven

Huevos: eggs

Jabalí: wild boar. A popular form of game, wild boar is usually served in a stew; it is particularly delicious with figs.

Jabugo: air-dried serrano ham from the Andalucían highlands.

Jamón: ham

Al jerez: cooked with sherry

Jerez de la Frontera: the city in Andalucía where sherry is produced. In Spain, sherry is known as vino de Jerez (see page 117).

Judía: bean. All shapes and colors of beans are used in a variety of dishes, more often dried than fresh.

Leche: milk. Spain's dairy industry is centered on the Picos de Europa, the picturesque inland mountain range that extends into the regions of Asturias and Cantabria.

Lengua: tongue. Lamb's, pig's, calf's and ox tongue are equally popular and prepared in a variety of ways.

Lentejas: lentils. Spain is one of the leading producers of this pulse, cultivated worldwide. Lentils are nourishing and easy to digest, and much used by Spaniards in dishes such as stews.

Limón: lemon (see page 85)

Málaga: sweet dessert wine

Manchego: ewe's milk cheese from La Mancha (see page 75)

Manzana: apple; popular also in cooked dishes, for example with poultry

Manzanilla: extremely dry sherry produced in the town of Sanlúcar de Barrameda. Its unique salty flavor is due to the proximity of the vineyards to the Atlantic Ocean.

Marinade: a seasoning mixture to coat or soak meat or fish before cooking in order to tenderize or impart flavor. A wet marinade is usually made from oil, herbs, vegetables and seasoning mixed with wine, vinegar or lemon juice; a dry marinade consists of a mixture of salt, herbs and spices.

A la marinera: food cooked in a white wine sauce

Mariscos: seafood

Mejillones: mussels

Melocotón: peach. Peaches in red wine are a favorite Spanish dessert.

Melón: melon. One of Spain's favorite fruits although it ids actually a vegetable.

Membrillo: quince

Menta: mint. The finely chopped leaves of this tangy herb add flavor to sauces, salads, and vegetables.

Merluza: hake. Popular in northern Spain and Portugal, the hake is related to the cod, and has delicate white flesh. It is often sold in steaks and is used in stews.

Morcilla: Spanish air-dried blood sausage. Good fried served as tapas, and added to stews.

Naranjas: oranges. Cultivated mainly in the huge orange groves around Valencia and Seville, oranges are used in both sweet and savory dishes in Spain.

Oloroso: rich, strong dessert sherry, varying in color from deep gold to brown

Paella: Spain's most famous rice dish, a colorful combination of meat, seafood, vegetables, and rice, cooked together and served in a large, two-handled pan.

Pan: bread

Patatas: potatoes. The Spanish national passion, often fried or made into tortilla de patatas, potato omelet.

Pato: duck

Pavo: turkey

Perejil: parsley. Spanish cooks prefer the flat-leaved variety, which has a rather milder flavor than the crinkly type.

Pescado: fish. Spain, surrounded on three sides by the sea, is renowned for its great variety of fish dishes.

Pichón: pigeon, squab

Pimentón: paprika, available in mild to very hot versions. Hot paprika is used sparingly, because although Spanish food is strongly seasoned it is not over-poweringly hot.

Pimienta: pepper (from peppercorns)

Pimiento: red green pepper

Piña: pineapple

Pincho: kabob. Meat kabobs, usually made with lamb or pork, are a popular barbecue food.

Plancha: grill or griddle

A la plancha: cooked on a hot, oiled griddle. In Spanish cuisine, fish, seafood, and meats can all be cooked this way.

Plátano: banana

Pollo: chicken

Pulpo: octopus

Queso: cheese. Spain has many fine cheeses, a number of which are served as appetizers.

Ragout: a well-seasoned stew of meat, poultry or fish

Rape: monkfish or angler fish; a firm, delicately flavored fish found in the northern coastal areas of Asturias and Cantabria

Render: to refine, or melt, the pure fat out of meat or poultry fat and tissues. Rendered fat, especially pork or goose, is used for cooking.

Riñones: kidneys. Usually prepared in a sherry sauce and served as an appetizer or entrée.

Romero: rosemary. This herb grows wild in many parts of Spain, and is used generously to season fish dishes

Sal: salt

Salmón: salmon. The wild mountain rivers of the Basque Country and Navarre are full of salmon, whose flesh is firmer and leaner than farm-bred specimens

Salsa: sauce

Salt cod: see bacalao

Sangría: red wine punch. To make, slice 1 untreated lemon, 1 untreated orange and 1 peach, and place in a jug. Sprinkle the fruit with 4 tbsp. sugar. Add 1 quart Spanish red wine. Chill well, then add 2 cups sparkling mineral water, and ice. Serve immediately.

Serrano: cured ham similar to Italian prosciutto (see page 108)

Seville orange: bitter orange, often used to make marmalade

Sidra: sparkling cider, a specialty of Asturias in northern Spain, where it is used in cooking and often replaces wine with a meal

Sobrasada: soft pork sausage from Majorca, similar to chorizo and often used as a spread

Sopa: soup. Hot and cold soups play an important role in Spanish cuisine; each region has its traditional recipes.

Tapas: appetizers – usually a mixed selection is served

Tocino: bacon

Tocino del cielo: "Bacon from heaven," Andalusian dessert made from sugar and egg yolks

Tomillo: thyme. Together with parsley and rosemary, thyme is one of the most widely used herbs in Spanish cookery. It is an essential ingredient of many lamb and game dishes.

Torta: cake, tart, or pie

Tortilla: omelet. One of the mainstays of Spanish cuisine, endlessly varied and served hot, warm or cold.

Trevélez: hard, air-dried serrano ham, named after the town of the same name in the Sierra Nevada

Trucha: trout. The mountain rivers of the Basque Country and Navarre produce particularly fine trout.

Truss: to secure the wings and legs of a bird against the body. This can be done by tying or sewing them with cotton or kitchen thread or string. The wings may also be tucked back under the bird.

Turrón: celebrated nougat from Jijona

Vieiras: scallops; a Galician specialty, usually prepared with garlic, parsley, and bread crumbs

Vinagre: vinegar. Sherry vinegar is very popular in Spain. Highly acidic, it should be used only sparingly; red wine vinegar can be used instead.

Yemas: candied egg yolks, a rich dessert created centuries ago by nuns in the bakeries of Andalucían convents

Zanahoria: carrot

Zarzuela: seafood stew from Catalonia, named after zarzuela, a traditional Spanish style of operetta.

CONVERSION CHART

These figures are not exact equivalents, but have been rounded up or down slightly to make measuring easier.

Weight Equivalents

Metric	Imperial
15 g	½ oz.
30 g	1 oz.
60 g	2 oz.
90 g	3 oz.
125 g	¼ lb.
150 g	5 oz.
200 g	7 oz.
250 g	½ lb.
350 g	¾ lb.
500 g	1 lb.
1 kg	2 to 2¼ lb.

Volume Equivalents

Metric	Imperial
8 cl	3 fl. oz.
12,5 cl	4 fl. oz.
15 cl	½ cup
17.5 cl	6 fl. oz.
25 cl	8 fl. oz.
30 cl	1 cup
35 cl	12 fl. oz.
45 cl	1½ cup
50 cl	16 fl. oz.
60 cl	2 cups
1 liter	35 fl. oz.

Cover: A varied selection of appetizers and generous glasses of Manzanilla sherry await guests at a tapas party. On offer are Moorish-style Pork Fillet Kabobs (page 39), Air-dried Chorizo Sausages, green and black olives, Pearl Onions in Sherry Vinegar (page 33), Marinated Anchovies (page 47), and Marinated Red Peppers (page 34), accompanied by crusty white bread.

Published in the United States by
Thunder Bay Press
An imprint of the Advantage Publishers Group
5880 Oberlin Drive
San Diego, CA 92121-4794
www.advantagebooksonline.com

Published originally under the title
Küchen der Welt: Spanien
© Copyright 1993 Gräfe und Unzer Verlag GmbH, Munich

English translation for the US edition
© Copyright 1999 Gräfe und Unzer Verlag GmbH, Munich
American adaptation by Josephine Bacon, American Pie, London

Copyright © 2000 Advanced Marketing Services, Inc.

Library of Congress Cataloging-in-Publication Data.
Molino, Cornelia Rosales de.
Cuisines of the world: Spain/Cornelia Rosales de Molino. p. cm.
Includes index. ISBN 1-57145-259-1
1. Cookery, Spanish. 2. Cookery-Spain.
I. Title.
TX723.5.S7 M66 2000. 641.5946–dc21

1 2 3 4 5   00 01 02 03 04

Color reproduction by Fotolito Longo, Bolzano, Italy
Typeset by Satz + Litho Sporer KG, Augsburg, Germany
Printed and bound by Artes Gráficas Toledo S.A.U.
D.L.TO: 245-2000

GRÄFE UND UNZER

EDITORS: Dr. Stephanie von Werz-Kovacs and Birgit Rademacker
Sub-Editor: Angela Hermann
Designer: Konstantin Kern
Recipes tested by: Renate Neis, Marianne Stadler
Production: Esta Denroche
Cartography: Huber, Munich
Color Illustrations: Bengt Fosshag

NORTH AMERICAN EDITION:
Managing Editor: JoAnn Padgett
Project Editor: Elizabeth McNulty

Cornelia Rosales de Molino, the author, was born in Jerez de la Frontera, sherry capital of Spain, and even as a child enjoyed spending time in the kitchen. Now a food journalist living in Madrid, she is the author of several cookbooks. She has chosen only the most authentic Spanish recipes for this book.

Foodphotography Eising Pete A. Eising and Susanne Eising specialize in food and drink photography and work closely with a food photographic agency operating in Germany and Switzerland. In addition to cookbook publishers, their clients include publishers, advertising agencies, industrial concerns, newspapers, and magazines. The food and props stylist for this volume was Martina Görlach.

Bengt Fosshag studied graphic design in Offenbach, Germany. Since 1983, he has worked as a freelance illustrator in a wide variety of styles. The props and the illustrations for this book are the result of his frequent visits to Spain over a period of more than 30 years.

Picture Credits

All photographs by *Foodphotography Eising* unless indicated below.

Cover. Graham Kirk, London. 4, top (2) and left, below center (market stall, Cadaqués, Costa Brava; castle, Sierra Nevada; traditional dress, Jerez de la Frontera feria): Gregor M. Schmid, Gilching, by Munich. 4, left, above center and bottom left (Corralejo beach, Fuerteventura; coastal mountains, Tenerife): Thomas Stankiewicz, Munich. 4, bottom right (Sitges wine festival): Martin Thomas, Aachen. 5, top (wrought iron balconies, Seville): Thomas Stankiewicz, Munich. 5, center (La Giralda, Seville): Gregor M. Schmid, Gilching, near Munich. 5, bottom (Ampurias, near L'Escala, Costa Brava): Martin Thomas, Aachen. 8/9: Thomas Stankiewicz, Munich. 10, 11: B. Barajas, Bildagentur J.D., Munich. 12, top: Thomas Stankiewicz, Munich. 12, bottom: Spanish Tourist Office. 13, 14 (2): Martin Thomas, Aachen. 15: Thomas Stankiewicz, Munich. 16, top: Spanish Tourist Office. 16, bottom and 16/17: Werner Neumeister, Munich. 18: Martin Thomas, Munich. 19 (2): Armin Faber, Mühlheim. 20, top and 21, bottom: Thomas Stankiewicz, Munich. 20, bottom and 21, top: A.M. Gross, Bildagentur J.D., Munich. 22: Spanish Tourist Office. 23: A.M. Gross, Bildagentur J.D., Munich. 24/25: real bild, Klaus D. Neumann, Munich. 25 (2): Spanish Tourist Office. 26: Gregor M. Schmid, Gilching, near Munich. 27 (2), 29 (2): Thomas Stankiewicz, Munich. 28, top: Thomas Widmann, Regensburg. 28, bottom: Martin Thomas, Aachen. 50: A.M. Gross, Bildagentur J.D., Munich. 71: Fotostudio Teubner, Füssen-Horn. 85: ai aigner impuls, Gottfried Aigner, Munich. 128: real bild, Klaus D. Neumann, Munich.